Perfect English

Perfect English

Ros Byam Shaw

with photography by **Chris Tubbs**

RYLAND
PETERS
& SMALL

LONDON NEW YORK

Dedicated to my mother, Margery Byam Shaw, whose generosity, knowledge, and "eye" are apparent in every room of my house.

Senior designer Toni Kay
Senior editor Clare Double
Location research Emily Westlake
Production Gemma Moules, Sheila Smith

Art director Anne-Marie Bulat
Publishing director Alison Starling

First published in the
United States in 2007 by
Ryland Peters & Small
519 Broadway, 5th Floor
New York, NY 10012
www.rylandpeters.com

10 9 8 7 6 5 4 3 2

Library of Congress Cataloging-in-Publication Data

Byam Shaw, Ros.
  Perfect English / Ros Byam Shaw ; with photography by Chris Tubbs.
    p. cm.
  Includes index.
  ISBN-13: 978-1-84597-345-2
  ISBN-10: 1-84597-345-3
  1. Interior decoration--England. I. Tubbs, Chris. II. Title.
  NK2043.B93 2007
  747.0942--dc22

                2006034661

Printed in China

CONTENTS

Introduction   6

PART ONE: PLAIN ENGLISH   12

Model Manor   14
Farmhouse Chic   22
Back to Basics   28
A Simple Retreat   36
Plain English Design Elements   42
Plain English Finishing Touches   44

PART TWO: ENGLISH ECCENTRIC   46

Purple Prose   48
Upstairs Downstairs   54
Beside the Seaside   62
A Movable Feast   68
English Eccentric Design Elements   76
English Eccentric Finishing Touches   78

PART THREE: ENGLISH ROSE   80

Tudor Restoration   82
Artist in Residence   90
Preserving the Fabric   96
Material Wealth   104
English Rose Design Elements   110
English Rose Finishing Touches   112

PART FOUR: ENGLISH
COUNTRY HOUSE   114

Reviving the Past   116
Elizabethan Jewel   124
A Stately Cottage   130
Country Legacy   136
At Home in History   144
English Country House Design Elements   150
English Country House Finishing Touches   152

PART FIVE: CLASSIC ENGLISH   154

Small and Beautiful   156
Singular Style   162
Classical Illusion   168
A Well-balanced Arrangement   176
Classic English Design Elements   182
Classic English Finishing Touches   184

Directory   186
Credits   188
Index   190
Acknowledgments   192

INTRODUCTION

Style is notoriously more difficult to describe than to recognize. Choosing the houses to be photographed for this book was as pleasurable as picking chocolates from a lavish box. Open it at any page and you would probably guess without reading a word that you were looking at an English house. But I found myself uncharacteristically tongue-tied when asked to sum up in a few words the style they represent.

In fact, one of the most significant links between these houses is not immediately apparent, because it is more a question of what has *not* been done to them, both structurally and in terms of decoration. Not one has been professionally decorated (with the exception of Endsleigh, which is a hotel and qualifies because its design is such a brilliant, and homelike, update of the English country-house style). True, there are houses belonging to interior designers, but Emily Todhunter, Justin Meath-Baker, and Diana Sieff claim almost in unison that, these being second homes and retreats from all things work-related, their interiors have been "thrown" and "cobbled" together with an emphasis on comfort and practicality.

Perhaps uniquely in a book about interior design, these rooms have not been over-designed. Instead they have tended to grow around their owners, accreting and shedding and being rearranged to suit. If the result is beautiful and stylish, it is because they have been put together by people who have a strong visual sense. This is in refreshing contrast to the current dominance of the label "designer," which now attaches itself to everything from bathrooms to teapots, and has an almost bullying effect, encouraging a style orthodoxy that has turned too many homes into show houses, their looks imported from pictures in magazines and weekends in luxury hotels. The houses here are the perfect antidote to this bland, copycat homogeneity, being more a form of self-expression than a means to impress, and offering as they do an intimate and often quirky reflection of their owners.

What we see in the arrangement of these rooms is not only the visual taste, but also the way of life of the people who inhabit them. Comfort is an essential ingredient. Just as the English prefer to dress for ease rather than glamour— compare the number of high heels clicking down an English sidewalk with those in France or Italy—so there is a prevailing English tendency to organize houses around the way they are lived in instead of allowing their design to become an imposition. A house without a capacious sofa, somewhere soft and squashy to sit with feet up amid the Sunday papers, would not have qualified for inclusion.

The English love of comfort is rivaled only by a fondness for history and nostalgia, so it should not be surprising that all the houses here are old, and what a realtor might advertise as replete with "period features." The youngest of them, that belonging to George Carter, is an octogenarian, while the oldest, Columbine Hall, dates back more than six hundred years. Several, including my own (see pages 82–89), have been comprehensively restored, stripped back to their bare bones, and re-clothed. But, again, it is the leaving well enough alone that distinguishes their finished state, since in every case the original fabric of the building, its character and patina, have been conserved and retained as far as practical and possible.

Rather than wishing to erase all traces of the past, the English have an incurably romantic attachment to it. Hew Stevenson and Leslie Geddes-Brown's dining-room ceiling is as gray as ancient underwear, stained with centuries of soot and pipe smoke. Justin and Eliza Meath-Baker's 17th-century beams and bare plaster molt onto their furniture. Even at Endsleigh, that luxurious country-house hotel, the original Regency wallpaper is so rubbed in places the pattern has almost disappeared. But, instead of painting, and sealing and re-papering them, these surfaces and their palpable evidence of hands and fires, damp and woodworm, are preserved and treasured. They may become the background for entirely modern furnishings—simple sofas, leather and chrome armchairs, sharp modern lamps— but the layering of time is apparent and enjoyed.

Roger Jones, whose nearly perfect flat appears on pages 176–181, astutely points out that "Imperfect English" might have been a more appropriate title. As head of antiques at Colefax and Fowler, birthplace of that quintessential English look, the English country-house style, he is one of the keepers of the John Fowler legacy. John Fowler was a professional decorator, but in a peculiarly English vein. His collaboration with Nancy Lancaster, the American heiress who in the 1940s bought the company that still bears his name, combined an English taste for the restrained, the pretty, and the unpretentious, with an American idea of domestic luxury. Both preferred interiors, however grand, that looked well used and lived in, both revered patina and rejected pomposity, both liked to use a casual mix of furniture gathered over time, and to dye or re-trim curtains rather than start from scratch. Descriptions of their work are often oxymoronic: "romantic disrepair," "studied carelessness," "humble elegance," "pleasing decay," "offhand perfection," an indication of the subtlety and depth of their approach.

Photographs of rooms they designed from the 1950s, 1960s, and 1970s look a little

dated now, with their round side tables heavily draped and loaded with trinkets, their pictures hung on ribbons and bows, and their density of objects. But the essentials of their style still seem very English and in fact inform all the houses on the following pages, however superficially different they may look. Nancy Lancaster compared furnishing a room to mixing a salad, insisting that sticking to one period of furniture, whether modern or antique, was never a success, and suggesting that every room should have in it something "warm and ugly." There are salads of all flavors here. All are delicious in their own way, and all as endearingly English as saying sorry when someone treads on your foot.

Ros Byam Shaw

PLAIN ENGLISH

"PLAIN" IS ONE OF THOSE SLIPPERY ENGLISH ADJECTIVES THAT CAN BE EITHER COMPLIMENTARY OR FAINTLY OFFENSIVE, DEPENDING ON ITS CONTEXT. USED TO DESCRIBE A STYLE OF SPEAKING OR WRITING, IT HAS A POSITIVE MEANING, DENOTING CLEAR, UNPRETENTIOUS COMMUNICATION. THERE IS A SENSE IN WHICH THESE SAME QUALITIES, PARTICULARLY THE LAST, CAN BE SEEN IN THE HOUSES ON THE FOLLOWING PAGES. NONE IS DEMANDINGLY MINIMAL AND NONE LACKS COMFORT, NOT EVEN THE COMFORT OF DECORATION, BUT ALL ARE PRACTICAL AND UNASSUMING. BY COINCIDENCE, ALL ARE SECOND HOMES, WHICH PERHAPS EXPLAINS THEIR EMPHASIS ON SIMPLICITY.

LEFT The rear elevation of this perfectly preserved miniature manor house overlooks its own valley. Philip and Catherine Mould have filled the gardens with 17th-century flowers and herbs and reinstated dewponds. Facing the front of the house is the original dovecote.

FAR LEFT The ground-floor kitchen opens straight into the garden. Once divided, the space is now opened up to make a room that combines cooking at one end centered on the Aga range, a long table for dining, and a seating area around the fireplace.

MODEL MANOR

Propped against a wall in the study of Philip and Catherine Mould's compact 17th-century manor house in Oxfordshire is a portrait of an Elizabethan lady, her soft, oval face framed by a ruff. "We thought we might find a place for her in a bedroom," Philip comments.

Tudor paintings are rare and very expensive, so this seems an unusually casual attitude, even from an art dealer as successful as Philip Mould. But lovely though she is, the Tudor lady is not what she seems. "The painting has lost its value," Philip explains, "because the original 16th-century face has been over-painted in the 18th century to make her prettier. I like her, but she's not particularly valuable."

Philip Mould has an eye for authenticity. He specializes in British portraits from the 16th to the 19th century and has made his name with a series of discoveries, most recently a portrait of Charles II that once stared down from a ceiling in Windsor Castle, and Gainsborough's "missing sister," a fragment of a larger work painted when the artist

ABOVE Where possible, the Moulds have bought furnishings contemporary in style or date with the house. The kitchen table is a plain Victorian piece, and the oak dining chairs are also Victorian but carved in late 17th-century style. The paneled sideboard against the wall is English, early 18th century.

ABOVE A battered buttoned
Chesterfield sofa stands against the
wall at the sitting end of the kitchen.
The leather is original and has acquired
a glossy, mottled patina of age. The
Moulds have been at pains to introduce
modern conveniences to this ancient
building with "as light a touch as
possible," even to the extent of choosing
an old-fashioned black telephone.

RIGHT The pair of leather armchairs
that flank the stone fireplace in the
kitchen have a medieval flavor, thanks
to their arched Gothic backs and rows of
close nailing, but in fact are early 20th-
century French. The preponderance of
leather, stone, and wood gives the
room an earthy, rustic feel.

was seventeen. "The reason I find this house so enchanting," he says, "is
that it has never been added to. Unlike the portrait, it remains intact, an
unadulterated example of early 17th-century vernacular architecture."

Philip characterizes his appreciation of the house as "visually
neurotic," but you would have to be hard-hearted and unromantic in the
extreme not to fall for its charms. Square and solid, it sits on the slope
of an intimate valley laced with water, some of which trickles down
the driveway. At the front its three storys with symmetrical mullioned
windows face a dovecote, but thanks to the steep pitch of the land, from
the back it rises a full four floors, like a benign and miniature castle with
its gabled staircase tower protruding in the middle.

Catherine Mould first spotted the house when it was advertised for
sale some years ago. At this point a second home in the country was a
plan for the future, but Catherine had found the house she wanted, and
she put the details in a drawer. Four years later, the couple were on
vacation and met some people who, it turned out, were going to stay at
the very same house. More recently, with a growing son, they decided
it was time to start country-house-hunting in earnest. Catherine showed

LEFT The front door leads straight into the main reception rooms. Ahead is a wide, wooden spiral staircase winding up to the bedrooms and down to the kitchen. When the Moulds bought the house, this floor was a single room. Originally there would have been two rooms, divided by the wooden walls of a screens passage. The Moulds partially reinstated this by commissioning one wall of linenfold paneling incorporating double doors, which now lead into a study on the left.

RIGHT The remaining space on this floor is the drawing room. Both rooms retain their carved stone chimney pieces, and both fireplaces are still in regular use, each with its pile of logs and essential wooden bellows. These rooms are hung with a choice selection of Philip Mould's finds.

the property search company her treasured brochure. To the amazement of all concerned, they announced that the house had just come onto the market. "Talk about being whacked on the head by the hand of destiny," Philip laughs.

Since buying the house, they have researched its history and found a record of a dwelling here in the Domesday Book. The house as its stands today was built in 1627. By modern standards it is not a particularly large house. There are two rooms on each of the three floors, with a bathroom in between on the two upper floors, and a single room on the first floor at the back. But its architectural moldings, its height, its staircase tower, and its dovecote were all significant status symbols.

As the centuries rolled by, it lost its status and became a farmhouse. By the middle of the last century, it was in such poor shape that it narrowly avoided demolition, saved by a visionary couple who revived it as a family home. Their restoration was sensible

and sensitive, but Philip and Catherine have taken it several steps further, by buying the land around the house, by creating a ravishing garden using 17th-century plants and structures, and internally by applying their "visual neurosis."

"Some of the most liberating moments were jemmying off plywood which had been used to cover rough plaster," remembers Philip. "With it came half a century of dust, desiccated mammals, and dead insects, but behind it the walls were untouched—the original patina of the house, perfectly preserved. It was a bit like swabbing a painting with acetone and finding another, older layer beneath."

Lighting, plumbing, and heating were addressed "with as light a hand as possible," and, on the floor where you enter the house at the front, they added a wooden screen wall of limewashed oak linenfold paneling, so subtly distressed it would take an eye as trained as Philip's to recognize it as new. These were the original reception rooms,

ABOVE There are two floors above the reception rooms, each with a symmetrical arrangement of two bedrooms with a small landing and a bathroom in between. The barley-sugar twist posts of this bed are late 17th-century Goan. There is no wall-to-wall carpet in the house. New oak boards were used where necessary, stained to match their older companions.

LEFT A bathroom is an unavoidable anachronism in a house of this date. The Moulds chose the old-fashioned comfort of Edwardian-style tubs and sinks and part-paneled the walls.

RIGHT At the top of the house are attic bedrooms fitted under the beams of the steeply pitched roof. This spare bedroom contains furnishings that span the centuries in a wide range of styles, from the heavily carved chest and section of paneling over the bed head, both early 17th century, to the Victorian metal bedstead itself, and the fanciful Victorian Gothic of the chair. Despite some ornate detail, plain walls, bare beams and floorboards, and the lack of curtains, conspire for an effect at the comfortable end of sparse.

as betrayed by their large stone fireplaces, and would once have been divided by just such screens.

"When you start to work on a house like this, the fact seems to pulsate through the area, and you find people emerging who have a passion for early architecture and who can advise and help. Local antique dealers Keith and Jane Riley have been invaluable, not just as a source of appropriate furnishing. They commissioned the screen and helped with all the woodwork, finding wide oak floorboards and reusing fragile original floorboards for windowsills. In the same way Charles and Jenny Norris appeared, who are experts in ancient horticulture and who have transformed the garden."

Philip loves English architecture and interiors for the same reason he specializes in British paintings. "Hogarth dismissed French portraiture as 'possessed of flutter' and you know exactly what he means," he says. "By contrast with the self-conscious polish of French and Italian portraits, there is something compellingly direct and unpretentious about British painting. I feel the same about this house. It does have a certain 'look at me' quality, but only in the most gentle way. I love its robust simplicity and the way it seems to grow out of its landscape."

ABOVE Across the landing from the double bedroom on the top floor is a bedroom with neat twin beds. Bedspreads here, and in all the bedrooms, are contemporary Indian patchworks, made from scraps of damask and brocade and hand-stitched for an effect that is more antique than modern. The painted and pedimented bedsteads, which are early 19th-century French, and the oval portrait of an 18th-century lawyer introduce a muted, classical elegance to this simple attic bedroom.

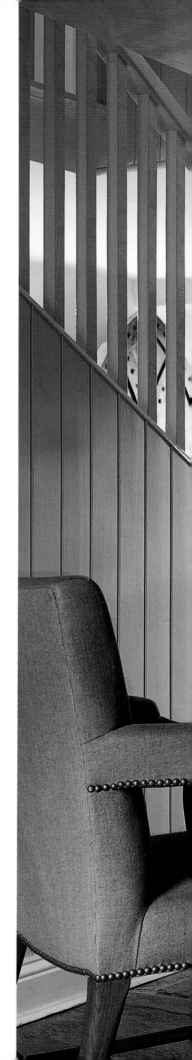

LEFT The kitchen was once a cowshed, attached at right angles to the original farmhouse, which has small, cozy rooms and low ceilings. In contrast, this is a large, lofty space, with a more formal dining area at the opposite end of the room to the huge, vintage range, which Diana Sieff describes as her "ultimate comfort zone." Probably the only things the cows would recognize are the exposed beams of the pitched roof. Antique wall cabinets supplement the built-in storage.

RIGHT The Sieffs opened up the entrance hall and built a new staircase, giving the house a much more spacious feel. The floor is new imitation flagstones. The faux-bamboo table is a long-term survivor, but the pair of light oak Arts and Crafts chairs and the plain 18th-century chest are newcomers.

FARMHOUSE CHIC

Simon and Diana Sieff are a glamorous and cosmopolitan couple. Their London-based company, Sieff, offers a full interior design service and sells a sophisticated mix of stylish antiques and modern upholstered furniture and accessories made to their own designs. Their showroom is an all-white warehouse, sparsely scattered with rectilinear sofas and chairs in neutral colors, spiced with the odd piece of old furniture—perhaps a curly 1920's metalwork console, or a plain French mirror. The look is fashionably pared down, elegant, chic, and more Continental than English in its seamless mixing of the old and the new.

It is not, however, as Diana explains, an inflexible "house style" ready to be imposed on her clients. "The most important thing when you are designing an interior for someone else," she says, "is to listen and to create the look that will make them feel most happy and at home, whether that is sharp modernity or traditional luxury." If you ask Diana Sieff to describe her personal style, her answer is immediate and

unequivocal. "I am completely into my comfort zone—my duvet, my bed, my pillows—and I love to be surrounded by antiques. Their connection with the past makes me feel calm. They seem to represent a quieter, less frenetic way of living." Although the Sieffs' flat in London is rather austere and furnished almost exclusively with pieces from the 1950s, which Diana describes as "hard-edged," their hearts, it

LEFT The elegant, airy living room was converted from a bike shed. Floor-to-ceiling French doors and matchboarding help to counteract the effect of the low ceiling. Sofas and lamps are modern designs from Sieff, which sit comfortably side by side with antiques. Diana is not generally a fan of curtains, preferring the more architectural effect of blinds, but has made several exceptions in this house, including these crewelwork curtains inherited from her grandmother.

RIGHT The dining end of the kitchen is dominated by a huge cupboard, bought for stock but so hard to move it will probably stay put. Giant antique wine bottles seem to float across its top like shiny glass balloons, and the equally over-scaled antler chandelier is from Anthony Redmile Antiques.

BELOW Between the hall and the living room is a sitting room painted in Farrow and Ball's Mouse's Back.

seems, and their most abiding tastes are located somewhere very different: on the edge of Exmoor, down a bumpy lane, surrounded by lush fields, hedges, and trees.

The Sieffs' home in the country is a small stone cottage, once a farmhouse, its plain, two-story façade enlivened by the simple Gothic details of drip lines over the windows and a front door with a pointed arch. The original house had two rooms on each floor, but it is joined at the back to old farm buildings that enclose a spacious square of courtyard, now a garden and sun-trap with an almost Mediterranean feel. The Sieffs have expanded the house into the former cowshed on one side to give themselves a large kitchen and dining room with a pitched, beamed roof, and into a former bicycle shed on the other side, now their summer living room.

"This is where we come to relax. This is

our sanctuary. And funnily enough, its interior has never been properly designed," smiles Diana. "Antiques come and go and the rooms seem to accept different pieces quite happily. Some things will always stay, like the huge old cupboard at the dining end of the kitchen, which we bought for stock but was a mistake because it is so enormous and heavy it takes eight men to move it. Or the crewelwork curtains in the summer living room, which are hand-me-downs from my grandmother." At the moment there is a pair of quirky Arts and Crafts chairs in the hall, and a plain 18th-century chest of drawers, but they may have gone in six months' time.

This casual turnover of furnishings helps to create the undecorated, almost impromptu look that Diana thinks is at the heart of English style. "I like to imagine that when I decorate a house for someone

RIGHT Downstairs the house is
expansive, thanks to the remodeling
of the cowshed and the bicycle shed,
but upstairs has not been extended
and comprises two small bedrooms
and a bathroom. Against a pure and
simple background of white walls,
bare floorboards, and minimal curtains
made by draping old linen sheets
over poles, unusual antiques like this
dressing stand with its pretty, integral
mirror look all the more striking.

I am only giving them a foundation. They will then add their own things,
things they like, things they are given, and gradually the interior will start to
layer. This is the charm of so many old English houses—everyone has made
a contribution over a period of years, and you will find incongruous things,
perhaps a funny old chair that someone has taken it into their head to upholster
in shocking pink, plonked down in the middle of a room, and it shouldn't, but
somehow it does, look great. It isn't an effect you can easily replicate when
decorating a house from scratch, but you hope it will happen as a room
matures. When antiques come and go in this house, you get that same feel
of it all being a happy accident rather than consciously designed."

The fact that any excess can always be sold probably helps to keep the house
free from clutter, such that it always stays at the spare and poised end of the
English style spectrum. "I am a fairly orderly person," Diana admits, "and
I don't like a lot of stuff around. I even prefer windows without curtains."

As for comfort, aside from her bed, Diana likes good plumbing, big sofas,
and an Aga in the kitchen. "You can't get more English than that," she asserts.

ABOVE LEFT The house is notably
free from clutter and knickknacks,
which Diana, who describes herself as
"very orderly," dislikes. However, she
is wedded to the comforts of pillows,
duvets, and fine linen, and both beds
in the house are piled with pillows.

BELOW LEFT In the bathroom, the
floorboards have been painted the same
shade of misty blue as the matchboard
paneling. The fine, dark lines of the
Victorian chair and quirky little side
table are silhouetted as if drawn in
charcoal on plain paper.

The main bedroom has the feel of a snug cabin, lined with painted matchboarding that covers the walls and the sloping ceiling. The contents of the room are minimal except for the lavish pile of pillows on the bed. What the room lacks in decoration is amply compensated for by a glorious view through French doors opposite the bed. These give access to a rose-clad balcony, which looks across meadows to the river.

LEFT The parlor to the right of the front door is one of the rooms given a makeover in the 18th century by a rich widow, who extended and modernized the farmhouse she inherited, covering the façade in brick, adding sash windows and, inside, fashionable corner fireplaces. The old brick floor has been painted as part of Justin and Eliza Meath-Baker's drive to banish rustic prettiness in favor of a leaner, more contemporary feel.

RIGHT The main living room was a kitchen and had an old Rayburn stove slotted into the wide, early 17th-century fireplace. The Meath-Bakers use the room as a living room and have furnished it with plain, modern sofas. The floor was covered with concrete, and they were planning to replace it with shiny resin until they discovered the original flagstones, crazed but intact, beneath. When a chunk of ceiling fell down, revealing decorated beams, they decided to strip off the rest of the ceiling.

BELOW RIGHT An austere expanse of plain gravel has taken the place of grass and flowerbeds.

BACK TO BASICS

The lane by the river gets narrower and more bumpy and then crumbles into a rough track through a field. Ahead is a small, square garden gazebo with a curving witch's hat of tiles topped by a finial. Beyond are the gables of a red-brick house—"a funny, peachy little place," as Eliza Meath-Baker describes it. For the past five years she and her husband, interior designer Justin Meath-Baker, have been visiting this house on the banks of the River Severn, directing builders, mending and tending it to make for themselves a simple, uncluttered country retreat. The house and its surrounding land once belonged to Justin's parents' estate. It was sold by his grandfather, then bought back and rented out.

ABOVE The kitchen is now a chic modern galley in the lean-to, which was once the Victorian scullery. This room is connected by a door and a large hatch to the adjoining dining room, which has a table flanked by chairs in conjoined rows of three, salvaged from an Edwardian theater in Edinburgh.

LEFT At the end of the table, "instead of a hutch covered in tasteful blue and white china," there is an old filing cabinet that belonged to Justin's grandfather displaying a collection of what he calls "naff cut glass."

Meanwhile, a fire had destroyed part of the house and the rest was in dire condition. "It was a dog's dinner," says Eliza. "It felt as though we were rescuing it, which, of course, was part of its appeal."

The original house was half-timbered, built around a central brick chimney stack in the early 17th century. A century later, the widow of a farmer lavished great expense on updating and aggrandizing the house, re-facing the exterior with brick, putting in sash windows and an elegant pillared doorcase and, inside, a new staircase and fashionable corner fireplaces. Fast-forward another hundred years, and this mini manor house was home to Jeremiah Hawkins, a famously eccentric Master of the Hunt who regularly swam across the river fully clothed with his pack of hounds until he and other local landowners clubbed together to build a bridge.

Justin and Eliza have stripped the house so comprehensively that even Jeremiah and the rich widow might be surprised by its structural austerity. "We are back to the skeleton of the house," says Justin. "The builders just giggled when we asked them to salvage the old elm floorboards, plane off their sides, and turn them upside down if necessary. As far as they were concerned, they were only fit for the bonfire. Now we have taken down the later plaster ceilings, when you are upstairs you can see through the floorboards to the rooms below, and we have to cover the sofas in drop cloths while we are away because a fine grit of old house falls on them through the gaps." A bit of dirt aside, the pared-down effect is what they were aiming for.

They found flagstones cracked into a wild mosaic under concrete in the living room, and decorated ceiling beams hidden under lath and plaster. "In summer, when all the doors and windows are open, the house feels so light and airy it could almost be floating," says Justin. Occasionally, it literally sits in the water. "Every ten years or so, the river rises up the bank and floods the house. It's another reason for keeping it plain and rather empty," he admits.

Justin claims that Eliza is "the austere one," while he "can't help collecting things." Both agreed that

Another corner fireplace is a legacy of the rich widow and her fashionable updatings. Above it hangs a painting by Eliza Meath-Baker, as restrained as her taste in interior design. Dishes and glasses are what Justin describes as "a funny mix of secondhand bits and pieces, because there's no point in being precious about a house that you have to leave empty some of the time."

ABOVE LEFT All the upstairs bedrooms retain their original wide elm floorboards. On the second floor the rooms below can be spied on through the gaps between the planks, where downstairs ceilings have been stripped back to the beams. A selection of vintage toys in the youngest son's bedroom fits nicely with the spare, tasteful aesthetic of the house.

ABOVE RIGHT Rooms on the second floor are on slightly different levels, giving the house a quaint, rambling feel. Looking from the spare bedroom across the landing, the main bedroom is a couple of steps lower.

LEFT A red metal sofa brings a flourish of exotic glamour to the spare bedroom, where a corner cupboard reflects the corner fireplace opposite.

RIGHT The main bedroom has windows at each end and an early 18th-century fireplace with a later cast-iron range. The fireplace is at least a century older than the beams, which were exposed by Justin and Eliza and are part of the original early 17th-century fabric of the house. The ornately carved chairs, "dodgy early 20th-century fakes we found in Warminster," make a striking pair, their complicated, three-dimensional curves in pleasing contrast with the plain, structural woodwork of the room's architecture. The large dishes on the hearth are creamers.

BELOW Justin made the bed himself around a mattress from Litvinoff and Fawcett. Its pale brown upholstery and the white sheets are echoed in the color of the beams and the white-painted walls. The floor lamps are Tolomeo by Artemide.

when furnishing this house one of their principles should be to reject anything that smacked of "country living," a design philosophy that Justin calls "urbe in rus." They took out the old Rayburn that others would have treasured, opened up the 16th-century fireplace, and made this former "farmhouse kitchen" into a living room, sparsely if comfortably furnished with two large sofas. Their kitchen is a stylish galley in the former scullery, with a door into the garden at either end.

In the dining room next door to the kitchen, there is no hutch hung with blue and white china, but instead an old filing cabinet topped by an arrangement of "naff cut glass." The study across the flagged hall from the living room, with its pretty glazed cupboards, has a single artwork on the wall, a framed patchwork of Pan paperback thrillers, collected by Justin and costing "a maximum of 20p each." The slightly eerie paintings

The two attic bedrooms are occupied by the older boys. The floorboards in this room were in a particularly bad state of repair. Some were turned over and re-planed, but others have been replaced with new wood. The new wood has not been stained to match the old, resulting in an attractive striped effect of pale and darker tones. A vintage filing cabinet makes a neat bedside table.

of birds in other rooms are the work of Eliza, who paints and exhibits as well as looking after their three boys. "I would really like to have used more modern furniture," says Justin, slightly wistfully, "but old furniture is cheaper. To some extent the interior has been designed by default—like the nasty glass basin in the bathroom, which was a reject from a job."

Aside from the washbasin, the bathroom is perhaps the closest they have come to rural minimalism. Cream rubber flooring sweeps across the floor and curves up the walls, between the rough ceiling beams, over the apex, and down the other side, while a bathtub sits, white and pristine, in the middle. "It's practical, and a little bit spartan, and a funny mix, like the rest of the house," Justin comments.

Their next plan is to re-roof and convert the adjacent barn, built, at the beginning of the 19th century, unusually close to the house so that Jeremiah could be near his hounds. "We want to make it into a space for the boys, so they can hang out there and have friends to stay without being under our noses. We were thinking of something quite radical, but then I found some old trusses on eBay that were such good value I had to buy them. That's what I mean by design by default." But, as Justin says, "it's easy to spend a lot of money," and much more difficult, and creative, to do something clever with what comes to hand.

ABOVE In the top-floor bathroom, with its sloping, beamed ceiling, there is a particularly bold juxtaposition of sleek, contemporary fixtures with the textured, weathered shell they occupy. The flooring of smooth, cream rubber tiling curves around where the roof meets the floor and flows up to the ceiling, making the room the most obvious example of Justin and Eliza's "typically perverse" aesthetic ideal, which they announce as "urbe in rus."

A SIMPLE RETREAT

Emily Todhunter's work as one half of the interior design team Todhunter Earle is often featured in glossy magazines. She has a way with expensive finishes—leather, glass, silver leaf—and an eye for putting the antique and the contemporary together to create rooms that are sleek, sophisticated, and timeless. This is Urban Emily. But there is another Emily, who doesn't get quite as much coverage.

"I like sophistication in town," says Emily, "but when we go to the country at weekends and in the holidays I want something else. I want to feel totally relaxed. I don't want to worry about muddy boots and wet clothes and dirty fingermarks and set mealtimes. I want to let go of all that city stress." The place where Emily, her Greek husband Manoli, and their three children retreat to from London is on the edge of a grouse moor in Cheshire's Peak District, in a wide, open landscape where the short-cropped grass of stone-walled fields meets heather and gorse.

Their house is on the Crag Hall shooting estate, which belongs to their friends the Earl and Countess of Derby. It was built as the gamekeeper's lodge and a couple of cowsheds at one end of a cobbled stableyard. "You open the door from the yard," says Emily, "and opposite, across the hall, is another door that opens onto the most glorious countryside. I heave a sigh of relief as soon as we arrive, and the children run straight outside, whatever the weather. In summer we swim in the river. We go for huge, long walks and we all ride. The house even has its own water supply. You do get the odd shrimp in the

ABOVE The house is designed to be practical—child-, dog-, and mudproof, and all the flooring downstairs is cork tiles. The entrance hall has a three-tier system of hooks: the top for hats, the middle for coats, and the bottom for children's coats. Hiking shoes and Wellington boots line up underneath.

LEFT The kitchen has a big, square table covered with a colorful Greek cloth, and French doors opening onto a terrace. Leading off the kitchen is a large playroom and utility room combined—"so I can watch the children while doing the ironing," says Emily. The pretty watercolors of fruit are by Emily's mother.

ABOVE The house was converted from a gamekeeper's cottage and cowshed, and because the buildings are listed as historic only minimal changes could be made to its exterior. The yard is terrace and turf, simple and low-maintenance, with a sheltering pine forest on one side and a view across fields to the moors beyond.

bathwater. The only neighbors are the estate workers who live in the cottages next door. It's the joy of total simplicity."

This pleasure in simplicity is the key to the way Emily has converted and furnished the house. The buildings are historically listed, and minimal changes were made to the exterior. Inside, Emily put in a second staircase. "The building is long and thin, so the bedrooms are all in a row," she explains. "The staircase gives guests some privacy." She also installed a raised fireplace in the living room, which retains its high windows from its days as a cowshed. "It's a little bit gloomy, but very cozy. Even in summer we often have a roaring fire, as it can get quite chilly in the evening."

For the sake of practicality, all the downstairs floors are cork tiles. "It doesn't show the dirt, and it has a warm feel underfoot. Upstairs I wanted wall-to-wall carpet for comfort and softness." Walls and

RIGHT Emily installed a raised fireplace with built-in storage for logs in the living room, which was converted from a cowshed and retains its original high windows. Colorful rugs, upholstery, and cushions add to the warmth of a blazing fire. Emily made the coffee table by cutting down the legs of an old kitchen table.

BELOW The informal feel of the house is enhanced downstairs by the way rooms flow one into the other. The hall opens into the kitchen and dining room. Its floor is brightened by a long, colorful kilim, which leads from the door past a cushioned bench with wicker baskets stacked neatly beneath to contain the overspill of shoes. Family photographs decorate the mirror.

One of Emily's essential ingredients for country comfort is a large bathtub, preferably one big enough to accommodate several tired children at once. This particularly capacious example is from *bathstore.com*, while the equally capacious chest of drawers was bought from Ray Coggins Interiors in Bradford-on-Avon. The chandelier adds a twirl of glittering glamour.

RIGHT Another of Emily's rural essentials is good-quality beds. The cottage has six bedrooms, which allows plenty of space for guests, who even have their own separate staircase. And, for warmth and softness, there is carpet everywhere upstairs in a pale, neutral wool and sisal mix. In this bedroom the headboard is covered in one of Emily's own fabrics, its leafy design echoed in the botanical prints she bought in a Paris flea market.

BELOW One of the spare bedrooms has an Arts and Crafts wooden bed and a stunning antique appliqué suzani as a bedcover, made in Uzbekistan. Another, more muted suzani hangs behind the bed. Walls throughout the house are painted bright white, "because it's so easy to repaint when and where necessary," but the rooms are far from cold and clinical, thanks to the vibrant colors and textures of furnishings and fabrics.

paintwork are white throughout. "You have not to mind that there are bubbles of damp and scuff marks, and it's easy enough to touch up." Emily's housekeeper made the curtains, all of which are unlined, using tablecloths from Greece and old French linen sheets. "And there are comfy, comfy beds and pillows and enormous bathtubs, which is exactly what you want after a long walk in the wind and rain," adds Emily.

As for furnishings, she claims they barely bought anything for the house. "We used things from the house we had in Gloucestershire and got other things out of storage. But I didn't want this house to look as though it had been decorated, and I like the way it's a bit thrown together." In truth, the decorator version of "thrown together" is rather more controlled and attractive

than it would be for anyone less schooled in the business of making rooms pretty. Against the background of white walls, the terracottas, mustards, blues, and purples of the upholstery, cushions, and rugs hum with warmth. Furniture is antique, of the sturdy, childproof variety, and there are old embroidered suzanis adding an exotic dash of color and pattern on the beds and used as wall hangings upstairs.

"Decoration needs to be appropriate to a building and its setting, and also to the way you use it and live in it, and that is probably a very English attitude. Professionally I may be better known for urban interiors," Emily comments, "but we also decorate a lot of houses for people in the country where something more robust and relaxed is required. What I really love is the contrast."

PLAIN ENGLISH design elements

Ever since the Reformation, when gangs of zealous vandals ransacked churches and cathedrals, hacking away the faces of idolatrous statues and whitewashing gaudy medieval frescoes, there has been a streak of the Puritan running through English taste. And the fact that our Protestant churches are so defiantly plain compared with the baroque extravagances of neighboring Catholic countries has helped to promote an enduring connection between simplicity and virtue. William Morris was making a moral as well as an aesthetic point when he rejected the decorative excesses of Victorian mass production with his famous admonition, "have nothing in your houses that you do not know to be useful, or believe to be beautiful." The recent fashion for more minimal, pared-down interiors has seen a renewed interest in the "honest" craftsmanship and simple lines of Arts and Crafts furnishing as promoted by Morris, and an increasing emphasis on the use of natural materials. The moral connotations have faded, but as a style of furnishing and decorating this no-frills approach is particularly appropriate for early and vernacular buildings with their architecture of weathered wood beams and floors, flagstones, and a minimum of architectural detailing. Plain can also mean versatile, as this is a style that works just as well for an industrial conversion or a workman's cottage.

• STONE FLOORS Very old houses tend to have flagstones, bricks, or terracotta tiles, often laid straight onto earth in ground-floor rooms. If you are lucky enough to have these in place, you will want to keep them. Alternatives are the composition "fake" flags used by the Sieffs, or a new stone with a bit of texture—very smooth limestone has a sleek, urban look, which may be too sophisticated.

• WOODEN FLOORS Bare boards have the right feel for this look, and it is well worth keeping as much of an original old floor as possible, even if, like the Meath-Bakers, this entails turning them over and re-sanding. Finding replacement new boards to match old, wide floorboards can be a problem, but it is possible to buy reclaimed floorboards if you want your new wooden floor to look as if it has always belonged.

• PLAIN WALLS are a key feature of the houses in this section of the book, and almost all are in shades of white. There has never been a

greater choice of types of paint—from authentic limewash to commercial latex—and there are enough different "whites," from the brilliant to the thoroughly grubby and ancient-looking, to satisfy the most exacting tastes.

• MATCHBOARDING is the most modest form of paneling, adding character and coziness to a plain room while keeping it simple. A less expensive way of getting the effect without using separate planks is to have sheets of composite board routed with V-shaped grooves in imitation of planks.

• WINDOWS Fully lined curtains using yards of fabric are too sumptuous for this look. Leaving a window bare of curtains emphasizes its architecture. Emily Todhunter used unlined Greek tablecloths for a fresh, simple effect, Diana Sieff used unlined antique linen sheets. If you require privacy or need to be able to shut out light, a plain shade is the least intrusive addition.

PLAIN ENGLISH finishing touches

If this style were to have a patron saint, it should probably be Jim Ede, whose Cambridge house, Kettle's Yard, was both home and art gallery, its plain white walls, bare floors, sparse furnishings, and mix of the antique with the contemporary an early prototype of the soulful minimalist style of decoration favored by so many artists and aesthetes since. Jim Ede was also a master of the well-placed *objet trouvé* with his much-copied spiral of pebbles, and pieces of driftwood posing as sculpture, on display in rooms that also featured works by Gaudier-Brzeska, Henry Moore, and Barbara Hepworth. Natural materials, whether in their natural state or crafted, smoothed, and polished into manmade furnishings, are key to this look.

• MODERN FURNITURE Of all the strands of English style featured, this one is the most accepting of contemporary furnishings. The simplicity of the modern sofas in the Meath-Bakers' living room suits their setting of bare stone floor, plain walls and exposed beams, while their clean, straight lines make a pleasing contrast with the irregularity of the crazed flagstones and time-weathered wood.

• OLD FURNITURE Perfectly plain, non-designer pieces from the first half of the last century are often better quality and less expensive than contemporary equivalents. Stripped of their dark, faux-antique varnish, plain oak furnishings from the 1920s and 1930s often look handsome when painted. Genuine early English furniture from the 16th to the 18th century is very desirable and expensive. Later reproductions, like the Moulds' kitchen chairs or the ornate chairs in the Meath-Bakers' bedroom, are a more affordable alternative.

• LEATHER upholstery, as long as it is old enough to be worn, glossy, and a little cracked with age, looks at its best in houses where natural materials predominate.

• POTTERY AND PEWTER For that sturdy, hand-crafted feel, pottery is better than china. Pewter, like leather, looks good with wood and stone, and, while pewter plates are decorative rather than usable, a pewter jug or tankard makes a nicely chunky vase.

• OBJETS TROUVÉS The windowsill on the stairs of the Moulds' house is a museum of fragments found in the garden, including a lead aeroplane, a Victorian penny, and shards of medieval pottery. If you live near the ocean, you probably bring home shells and stones and interesting bits of driftwood. "Found objects" carry with them a strong sense of time and place, and finding ways to display or use them can be very satisfying; large scallop shells make pretty soap dishes, for example, and pieces of pottery or pebbles can be made into mosaics to decorate a garden wall, while a string of stones with holes through them hung at the door is said to keep away witches.

• FABRICS Solid fabrics, stripes, checks, or weaves with a slightly ethnic feel are right for this pared-down look. Heavy antique linen sheets, or hemp, or old feed sacks in unbleached linen make very chic upholstery with a suitably rustic edge.

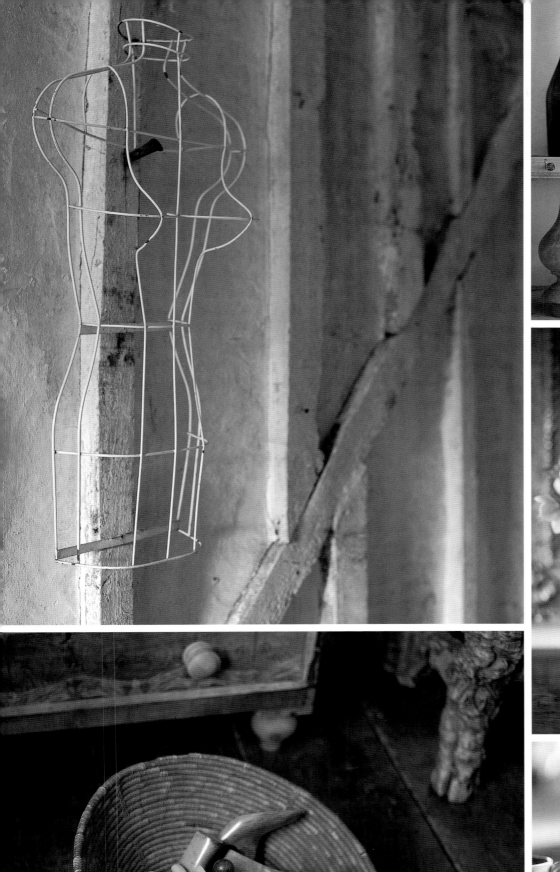

ENGLISH ECCENTRIC

THE WORDS "ENGLISH" AND "ECCENTRIC" GO TOGETHER LIKE "FISH" AND "CHIPS." AS LIGHT RELIEF FROM A NATURAL RETICENCE, THE ENGLISH ARE ENCHANTED BY THE SLIGHTLY DOPEY AND FONDLY TOLERANT OF MISFITS. THE GENUINE ECCENTRIC APPEARS INNOCENTLY IMPERVIOUS TO CONVENTION AND CONFORMITY. TO THIS EXTENT, AN ECCENTRIC INTERIOR IS MORE IMMUNE THAN MOST TO THE PRESSURES OF FASHION AND THEREFORE A MORE HONEST EXPRESSION OF INDIVIDUALITY. ALTHOUGH FAR FROM EXTREME EXAMPLES OF ECCENTRICITY, THE HOUSES IN THIS CHAPTER OWE MUCH OF THEIR CHARM TO THE VERY DIRECT WAY IN WHICH THEY REFLECT THEIR OWNERS.

PURPLE PROSE

ABOVE All the floorboards, including the stair treads, are covered with specialized floor paint. The lightbulb is decked in Tord Boontje's "Garland" of sparkling sheet metal from Habitat.

Raffaella Barker wanted her kitchen to be like a tulip and her living room to be like Biba, not a conventional approach to the decoration of a Victorian rectory in the middle of fields and woodland. "I had driven past this house many times," Raffaella says, "so when I heard it was available for rent I was very excited. I love its position in its own landscape, looking down over the most ravishing bluebell woods."

"It feels so romantic, as if a knight in shining armor might come galloping down the road at any moment. But it was very daunting to take on. It had been lived in for years by a tenant farmer and was full of swirly carpet. There was no heating and it was in bad repair."

While the landlord agreed to deal with the structural issues, Raffaella was determined to make the interior decisions herself. "I had very little in the way of furnishings, and it's quite a big house, so I decided to fill it with color. But I needed some advice so I asked Annabel Grey, who has a brilliant eye for color, if she would help me." Raffaella knew Annabel's style from her work as

LEFT The living-room walls are painted in dusty purple limewash, a type of paint that has a more three-dimensional, textured effect than ordinary latex. Above the antique leather chair hangs a painting by David Gryn that Raffaella bought when she was twenty, a wash of color that might have inspired the room itself. In fact, Raffaella's inspiration was Biba.

RIGHT Set against the dusky backdrop of the walls and woodwork, the bright oranges, pinks, and reds of the upholstery, leather floor cushion, and carpet acquire an almost neon glow. Styles and periods of furnishing in this room are a carefree mix ranging from the 19th-century French table to the modern flower lamps by Helena Christensen from Habitat. The painting is by Endellion Lycett Green.

an interior designer at Voewood House, an Arts and Crafts mansion by E. S. Prior in the same part of Norfolk, and from Annabel's own cottage (see pages 90–95).

Knowing that Raffaella wanted strong, even clashing color, Annabel picked a generous mixed bunch of flowers from her garden so they could look at them together and decide which particular colors Raffaella wanted for each room and how they would relate to one another. Sweet peas and poppies and lavender and their leaves, as well as tulips, became the cue for the colors of walls—and floors and doors and baseboards.

From the outside the house is quirky and ecclesiastical, a Victorian version of Gothic with an arched front door, pointed gables, and a forest of extremely tall octagonal chimneys, each topped by a flat crown of spiky terracotta stars. It looks like the setting for a Barchester Chronicle, or an Edwardian tea party.

So, if you enter through the back door, past the pecking bantams and Raffaella's vintage red Jaguar, the kitchen comes as quite a shock. Walls are a vibrant pink, woodwork is glossy red, the floorboards have been painted purple, and the table has a shiny red Formica top. "I suppose it is quite extreme," admits Raffaella, "but I love it. The colors are just so delicious."

A doorway, recently created, leads into the dining room and a continuation of the pinks, reds, and purples. Colors in the hall are more subdued; a dusky purple for the floorboards and the wooden treads of the pretty curving staircase, and a duskier shade, like mushroom soup, on the walls to dado level. Leading off the hall, opposite the dining room, the living room is a medley of smoky, Biba-esque purples.

While the color schemes downstairs are rich and warm, upstairs the feel is more airy, with walls and woodwork painted in blues and pale blues, so that climbing the

ABOVE One of Raffaella's more radical interior adjustments was to transform the former pantry into a Moroccan-style wet room and shower next door to her study. In other respects the downstairs layout of the house is a conventional one, with dining room and living room flanking the entrance hall and the kitchen at the back.

LEFT The kitchen has a jolly, almost fairytale feel with fire-engine red paintwork, bright pink limewash walls, and a purple painted floor. The mantelpiece displays objects that range from kitsch to curiosity, including a bust of Dante, red plastic roses, a boxed scorpion, and a miniature cricket bat.

OPPOSITE The dining room mirrors the living room at the front of the house, but rather than a formal space, Raffaella has made it a comfortable extension of the kitchen by knocking a wide doorway through from one into the other. Having ripped out the ugly fireplace tiling, Raffaella commissioned artist Annabel Grey to reclothe it in plates and a mosaic of broken china. The curtains are similarly unconventional, made from cozy mohair blankets sewn together and edged with grosgrain ribbon.

stairs from the shady hall feels like climbing to the top of a tree and seeing the sky. Raffaella's three children were allowed to choose their own schemes: the youngest girl has feather-trimmed curtains, while the older boys have gray and red, and blue and orange, rooms respectively.

Although Raffaella claims to have very few possessions, the ones she does have are as striking as the paint that is their background. A few items came from her last house, but most she has bought, cheaply, from markets and antique shops. Economy has been the mother of some inspired invention. The dining-room curtains are mohair blankets sewn together, cozy and unlined. In the same room, the fireplace has been "tiled," by Annabel, with a flowery mosaic of china plates.

Nothing about the interior of this house is conventional. The pantry has been converted into a walk-in shower, and even the study next door is not really a study. "I find I can't write in it," says Raffaella, whose novels line up on the shelves. "I prefer to write in my bedroom, or at someone else's house. This house is for living in."

ABOVE The stairs lead up to a generous landing, which had previously been walled in to make an extra bedroom. The light, airy feel of this space is emphasized by the transition to paint colors in shades of blue and gray, like clouds and sky. In Raffaella's bedroom the pale, almost ethereal color scheme continues.

LEFT Raffaella's bedroom has boudoir glamour with its pale walls, pale painted floor, and large French-style bed with distressed white paintwork. The frilly 1930's mirror above the fireplace reflects pretty glass wall lights, and the dressing table is also mirrored for extra glitter. As in the rest of the house, most of the contents of the room were bought cheaply and secondhand.

FAR LEFT Raffaella was worried that the shades of lilac she chose for her bathroom might make the room feel like "a Barbie bath set." In fact, the space feels calm and sophisticated. The roll-top tub was originally found in a junkyard and came from Raffaella's old house, because the new owners did not want it. Raffaella's collection of shell-covered boxes is also housed here.

LEFT The curtains in the upstairs living room were made from cheap yellow fabric with a black anthemion stenciled border designed by Alan. The front part of the room spans the width of the house and is lit by tall sash windows, which reach almost down to floor level. The floorboards are covered by rush matting and rugs.

RIGHT Like other rooms in the house, the living room serves more than one function, as sitting and reception room, and also as a study for at least three members of the household. The walls are painted in pink distemper, the ceiling in blue. Although decorator John Fowler used to recommend no fewer than seven coats of tinted distemper, Alan thinks they only managed three or four. Susanna was responsible for stripping years of paint from the delicate crown molding.

BELOW The enormous cupboard at the left of the fireplace is storage for the Judd Street Gallery Pattern Papers produced by Alan and Susanna when they ran an art gallery in the ground-floor shop. The papers feature the work of artists such as Enid Marx, Eric Ravilious, and Edward Bawden.

UPSTAIRS DOWNSTAIRS

"This house is pure mid-1980s," announces Alan Powers. As the house has a distinctly Georgian façade, its sash windows rising in three tiers above its arched front door, the remark is momentarily confusing. In fact, he is referring to the way it is decorated and the heyday of the New Georgian Handbook, *when aesthetes and conservationists, fired by nostalgia and undeterred by undesirable London neighborhoods, sought out 18th- and early 19th-century houses ripe for restoration. This was the era when Spitalfields was saved from dereliction and PhDs spent weekends picking paint off moldings.*

LEFT Although attracted by its age, size, and period features, not to mention its relatively low price, Alan and Susanna were of two minds about buying the house in the early 1980s because it is on a busy road. To live as far from the traffic noise as possible, they chose the back room on the third floor, originally a bedroom, as their new kitchen. The room has the informal feel of a living room, thanks to its mix of built-in cupboards and freestanding pieces. Open shelving displays some of their collection of old china. Everyday plates are wooden and stored in a plate rack above the sink.

RIGHT Some of the antique china is in use, some purely decorative. Luster mugs hold pencils and pens, a Victorian jug a selection of tools. The old blue enamel pots make attractive storage, and enamel ladles dangle ready to use.

Alan Powers knows his architectural and interior design history better than most. Trained as an art historian, he is currently Reader in Architecture and Cultural History at the University of Greenwich. He has also worked as a painter and illustrator, and has an impressive list of books to his name on design- and architecture-related subjects. And although his house might suggest an architectural bias toward the historical, he has had a long association with The Twentieth Century Society, becoming its first Caseworker in the early 1980s and now serving as a member of its Main Committee.

Alan and his wife Susanna bought this house on a busy road on the edge of Bloomsbury in 1983, when Alan joined a tour of prospective buyers and heard a builder suggest that "everything should be ripped out." Instead they kept it and mended it, including picking paint off molding, finding replacement fireplaces, and commissioning new sash windows. The house was built in 1816, and Alan believes the ground floor was converted into a shop at some stage in the 1850s.

Today the ground floor is still a shop, a bookshop, but for some years Alan and Susanna ran it as a gallery, renting it as an exhibition space to "friends and friends of friends." The gallery chimed with their enthusiasm for 20th-century "academic, narrative" artists. Although the gallery has now gone, this enthusiasm is obvious the moment you step into their narrow hall and start the journey up the old staircase to the third-floor kitchen.

ABOVE The kitchen retains its original fireplace, protected by a guard rail. Even in this functional room, every spare bit of wall is decorated with pictures. The table sits beneath the window, which overlooks the walled garden at the back of the house.

It is hardly surprising that a house belonging to a book editor, and a writer and academic, should be bursting at the seams with books. The room next to the kitchen, known as the "family room," is also a library, with a wall of dark-green-painted shelves and cupboards designed by Alan with a mirrored alcove at their center. More books are stored in bookcases inherited from Alan's grandfather, who lived in one of Britain's first flat-roofed Modernist houses.

RIGHT This same room, contrary to appearances, is Alan and Susanna's bedroom; the striped sofa is a convertible sofa. Any wall not occupied by books is hung with pictures by 20th-century artists, including paintings by Hermione Hammond and Winifred Knight. The model of a man about to leap from the fireplace was made by their son, William.

The journey is impossible without frequent pauses to stand and stare. The first showstopper is a four-seater Canadian canoe hanging from the ceiling in the hall, where its long, slim hull fits rather neatly. "We take it to Suffolk in the summer," says Alan by way of explanation. All the way up the stairs are 20th-century pictures and prints, every one worth a good look, some by Alan, and including works by John Piper, Edward Bawden, Eric Ravilious, and Alan Sorrell. Any remaining wall space has been commandeered for books. Books and pictures continue up to the fourth floor and into every room, with the exception of the bathroom, which has pictures but no books.

The back room on the third floor was chosen as the kitchen for its relative distance from the noise of traffic. The front room next to it is the "family room" and features a bookcase along one wall, designed by Alan, painted dark green and with a mirrored alcove at its center. There are also a sofa and a desk, a couple of armchairs, and more pictures, notably by Winifred Knight and Hermione

Hammond. Despite appearances this room doubles, or should it be trebles, as main bedroom and dining room. The sofa is a bed, made and unmade every morning and evening, and pushed aside to make space for a table when the room is used for entertaining. "It's proper 18th-century living," laughs Susanna, referring to the Georgian habit of putting up a table for a meal in whatever room seemed most convenient at the time.

On the floor above are the bathroom and two small bedrooms belonging to their children: Eleanor, who is studying medicine, and William, who is still at school and hoping to work in films. The bathroom apparently is where the children used to play. Conveniently the bathtub stands in the middle on feet, allowing a train track to pass beneath. "We used to pick our way across it to get to the washbasin," Susanna fondly remembers. Now you are more likely to find sheets of impenetrable medical study notes mounted on the wall.

As for the second-floor living room, which spans the house and reaches from front to back, this

LEFT For anyone interested in 20th-century art, climbing or descending the stairs is likely to be a slow process, as the staircase walls from the ground floor to the top floor are covered in a tight tessellation of pictures by artists such as Eric Ravilious, Alan Sorrell, John Piper, and Edward Bawden. Among them are drawings and watercolors by Alan himself, who trained as an art historian but worked for many years as a painter and illustrator, as well as a writer.

BELOW LEFT On the landing opposite the bathroom are two luster teacups, part of a collection started by Alan and Susanna when they first met. An Arts and Crafts repoussé copper mirror hangs above an oak chest of drawers from the same era, with repoussé copper drawer fronts.

"seems to be my office at the moment," says Alan. There is also a desk for William, where he is making one of his slightly sinister movable figures, to be used in a film. (Other members of this faceless tribe cavort on the grate of a fireplace or peer out from between books.) A third table is piled with medical textbooks. What with the birdcage housing the stereo, a quartet of armchairs around the fireplace, and a cupboard stacked with the beautiful, printed Judd Street Gallery Pattern Papers, which are still for sale while stocks last, there isn't room for much else. Sensibly, Susanna works elsewhere, for the Folio Society—conveniently just around the corner.

"Nothing has been chosen for the house, or planned," says Alan. "It's a working compromise of things I inherited from my father, who was an architect, and things we have bought or otherwise acquired." This lack of contrived "decoration" and the way the house, its layout, and the contents so unselfconsciously reflect the tastes and habits of its occupants, are precisely what make it so charming and so unmistakably English.

The top-floor bathroom is decorated with schools prints and an early "cubist" work by Alan, aged seventeen. When younger, the two children used it as their playroom, running train tracks under the tub and continuing the household trend for multipurpose rooms.

LEFT The kitchen was gloomy with "lurid green" built-in cupboards. Rather than dump them, the Pruskins repainted them pale Wedgwood green to match their china. The oak chairs, table, and sideboard are all Heal's 1910, and the set of prints above the sideboard are 1930's Dutch, designed for schools. The Victorian glass dome enclosing a miniature landscape looks almost modern here.

RIGHT The living room opens into a conservatory and is furnished with things that "didn't fit anywhere else," including a large kilim-covered sofa from George Smith. The huge floor cushion is Arts and Crafts crewelwork; the second sofa is covered in fabric bought cheaply from a local market.

BESIDE THE SEASIDE

When Julia and Michael Pruskin's daughter Isadora was born in 1999, they found themselves hankering for somewhere they could escape that didn't entail hanging around in an airport. "We had both lived and worked in London all our adult lives, but I had always loved Southwold—it's such a pretty, old-fashioned English seaside place," Julia says. "During the week we are buying for the shops and need to be based in London, but Southwold on the Suffolk coast seemed an ideal place to look for a weekend and vacation house."

They first spotted the house they now own when they walked past it on one of many visits to Southwold and noticed furniture being carried out. It was on a street of shops and not particularly prepossessing, so when, a couple of weeks later, they saw it was for sale, they nearly did not bother to view it. "Thank goodness we did," says Julia, "because the moment we walked through the front door we loved it. It was such a surprise—big rooms and a slightly rambling, unexpected layout, and

ABOVE The shadow of an enormous beech tree in the yard falls across the back of the house. The projecting wing on the right is the old coach house, separate from the main house downstairs but connected upstairs and containing an extra bedroom and bathroom. The rambling internal layout was one of the attractions of the house.

ABOVE The staircase up to the large landing dates from the 1960s, when the house was divided into two. The Pruskins added the Victorian cast-iron spiral staircase to replace the ladder leading to the attic bedrooms.

LEFT Every room in the house contains at least one unusual find. In this room the most striking is the glass-fronted case of butterflies on a painted panorama, probably made for a museum at the beginning of the 20th century. The natural history theme is continued by the pair of screens, decorated with shells and seaweed preserved behind glass. Julia describes the Fulham Pottery vases, which add another collection to the room, as "breeding in captivity." The coved ceiling is just one of many architectural oddities in a house that has been altered many times over several hundred years, while the travertine floor, which continues into the hall and kitchen, is one of the few structural additions made by the Pruskins.

a beautiful garden at the back with a huge beech tree—the biggest tree we have ever owned. Even though the house is on a street in the middle of a town, it felt secret and hidden. And it's only five minutes' walk to the ocean."

Despite its unremarkable façade, it is a very old house, once a manor house. At some stage it was divided into two and has been altered, added to, and possibly even subtracted from over the years, making it difficult to unravel its architectural history. Michael and Julia did very little structural work. "The house was rather dirty and decorated in very strong and gloomy colors," Julia remembers. "But, just like a good piece of antique furniture, all it needed was a bit of buffing up." The buffing included new travertine floors in the hall, kitchen, and dining room downstairs, and a painted metal spiral staircase to replace the ladder leading from the large landing to the attic bedrooms.

Being antique dealers, it was second nature to Julia and Michael to keep and restore as many of the original fixtures in the house as possible. Kitchen

Julia says that they "keep trying to be minimalist, but can't stop ourselves buying things on impulse." The main bedroom has a simple, almost graphic quality, with the sweeping lines of the iron bed drawn against the plain walls, but it also contains highly decorative items such as the Victorian picture above the bed, which creates a geometric pattern from a collection of insects.

LEFT Plain, sturdy pieces from the late 19th and early 20th centuries make good-looking and practical bedroom furnishings, but each bedroom contains at least one remarkable item. In Isadora's room, the conversation piece is the wooden bedstead dating from the turn of the 19th century and heavily carved with pinecones like something from a woodland fairytale.

BELOW Being antique dealers the Pruskins are natural conservationists, preferring to restore old fixtures rather than replace them with new. Where possible, they kept bathtubs and basins and refurbished the 1950's faucets. In this bathroom they used beveled brick-shaped tiles for a period feel, and hung 1930's mirrors above the basin.

cupboards were repainted, the dark green range was refurbished, the butler's sink and teak draining board scrubbed, a cast-iron bathtub was encased in new panels, and even the "funny old" 1950's faucets stayed. As for furnishings, Julia says that they put lots of things in the house that "didn't fit anywhere else."

Julia and Michael's two London shops, the Pruskin Gallery on Kensington Church Street and their new premises in Notting Hill, always contain an interesting and covetable collection of the 20th-century furnishings that are their specialty, from Arts and Crafts oak, through glamorous Art Deco, to more wacky designer pieces from the 1950s, 1960s, and 1970s.

"One of the great things about having a shop," Julia admits, "is that it allows you to express more than one aspect of your taste. I can arrange an elegant, minimal store window and achieve an effect I could never manage at home. And the joy of having a second house with lots of space is that you can buy something just because you like it, then find a place for it. A lot of our customers are interior designers, and we often buy things for a particular scheme. The furnishings in Southwold have been gathered in a much more relaxed way and are a jumble of things we already owned and things we couldn't resist."

It is difficult to reconcile Julia's description of haphazard and impetuous buying with these attractive and balanced rooms. It is true that there are some odd conjunctions: a vibrant poster-size painting by René Gruau hangs on the stairs at the same height as a traditional brass chandelier; specimen butterflies

from a museum display flit across a painted landscape, with a collection of Fulham Pottery vases balanced along the top. In the living room, Julia covered the "bordello pink" upholstery of a secondhand sofa with chintz bought in a local market, and paired it with a kilim-covered couch and a giant Arts and Crafts embroidered floor cushion. "Absolutely nothing matches," she says cheerfully. "But here it somehow doesn't matter."

LEFT AND FAR LEFT The house dates from the early 18th century and has a prettily symmetrical façade in pale honey-colored stone. When Robin Eden first bought it, very cheaply, it was suffering from planning blight. Fortunately the main road, which would have divided the house from its backyard, was never built.

RIGHT The long table in the hall has a 17th-century top on new oak trestles. The lamp, not so long ago one of a pair, has a gessoed oak base and a shade of ikat silk made by Miranda.

A MOVABLE FEAST

The contents of Matthew and Miranda Eden's Wiltshire house are constantly on the move. You might not notice if you visited every day, but just as you can't help blurting out how much children have grown when you haven't seen them for a while, so it is a shock to find that something has disappeared from the house, usually something lovely, since you last saw it.

BELOW The original oak staircase with its slim balusters rises from the far end of the entrance hall. The front two rooms on either side of the hall are the living room and dining room. The door seen here next to the staircase opens into the back sitting room and opposite is a door leading into an informal dining room.

Fortunately, the loss is invariably made up for by the arrival of something else equally, if not more, lovely. For example, it was difficult to imagine a prettier bed than the four-poster in their bedroom, with its barley-sugar-twist painted metal posts and canopy of antique chintz. Until, that is, you see their new one, a gift from a friend on the move, antique dealer Peter Hone. Made by Colefax and Fowler for Nancy (later Lancaster) and Ronald Tree, it is hung with floral chintz so thoroughly faded the pattern has dissolved into the prettiest wisps of pink.

Inimitably stylish, Nancy Lancaster (who later bought Colefax and Fowler) preferred fabrics to look well worn and was known to leave new slipcovers outside for days until they were sufficiently weathered, a treatment that may well have been

LEFT The Edens refer to this informal dining room as the kitchen as it leads straight into the former scullery, which now houses the sink, range, and fridge. This room has a huge old fireplace and was the original kitchen, although the flagstones are new and were added by Matthew and Miranda. They replaced a layer of parquet over concrete, which in turn had replaced the 18th-century stone floor. Staring down over the table and its set of reproduction Lutyens chairs is a splendid lion with enormous paws, probably 18th century and painted on a blanket. A missing chunk was replaced with burlap by Robin Eden, who also painted in the lost piece of tail. The image of Rome on its left is a rare, early photograph dating from 1860.

RIGHT The working end of the kitchen was once the scullery. The Aga range had been used to boil up animal feed when Matthew and Miranda bought it secondhand. Sandblasted and re-enameled, it looks as good as new. The kitchen cabinets were made to the Edens' design by a local craftsman.

meted out to these very hangings. The bed was so tall it had to be cut down to fit Matthew and Miranda's bedroom, and the elaborate 18th-century finials that once graced its canopy sit on shelves downstairs like strangely desirable, moth-eaten sculptures. Despite pruning, the bed remains enviably elegant, and it is a relief to find that the barley-sugar-twist bed has moved across the landing to another bedroom.

Matthew and Miranda moved into the house when Matthew's parents, Robin and Catherine Eden, moved out. Robin Eden was an antique dealer, remembered by his clients as a gentleman of old-fashioned charm with an unfailing eye for the fine and the fascinating. Elizabeth Baer (see pages 96–103) credits him with launching her career in antique textiles when she bought a pair of chintz bedcovers from him. "I never realized how special they were until I saw a similar pair on the King's Road a few years later," she says.

Robin Eden also had an eye for a bargain, and the house itself was one of his best. Early 18th century, its central door and flanking sash windows arranged with dollhouse neatness, its only disadvantage and the reason for its irresistibly low price tag was the threat of a new main road due to be routed past its back door. That was in the 1950s, and the back door still opens onto uninterrupted backyard. The road faded in a filing cabinet, and Robin and Catherine built themselves a house in the vegetable garden, which they moved into nearly fifteen years ago to make room for Matthew and Miranda and their three children.

Matthew makes beautiful reproduction garden furniture, and has expanded it to make a successful business. He also inherited his father's taste and talent for spotting a clever purchase, and has never been able to resist buying antiques and selling them as his own sideline. For years the converted coach house and stable next to the house has contained a selection of unusual and covetable antiques, and Matthew can boast of having bought and sold curiosities and treasures as diverse as Ernest Shackleton's sled, D. H. Lawrence's bathtub, and Christopher Wren's copper ball from the top of Tom Tower. With both businesses now winding down, it is impossible to believe that Matthew won't continue to acquire things he "can't help buying" and then find himself selling them when he runs out of space.

While Matthew continues to deal, the house remains far from cluttered, presumably because people keep buying. With admirable restraint, Matthew and Miranda made very few changes when they first moved in. They put another coat of paint over the blue distemper in the living room but left the ceiling untouched in order to preserve the faint black smoke stains dating back to the days of gas

RIGHT The sitting room at the back of the house contains a choice of well-padded seating including an extra-large sofa piled with big cushions and this capacious Victorian armchair. The old upholstery, a faded linen floral, has been preserved and supplemented by plain linen, added by Miranda, who can make anything in fabric from blinds and curtains to lampshades and giant parasols. The painting behind is by a Victorian ancestor of Matthew's named Archie McGregor and is in the style of his contemporary, George Frederick Watts. The red tin bucket is used as a coal scuttle, but was designed as a fire extinguisher.

BELOW Matthew's parents painted this strange, geometric design on the landing wall—as Matthew remembers, "using very small brushes."

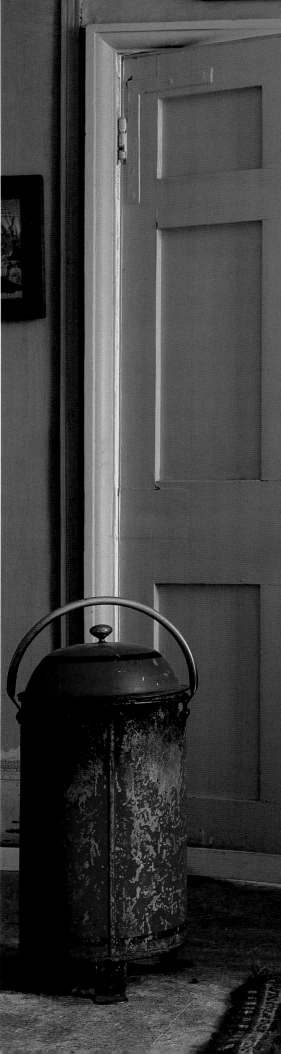

lighting. They took up a wooden floor in the back sitting room and found flagstones beneath, but they left the original William Morris wallpaper on the chimney breast. Also intact is the landing wall embellished with a strange if pleasing design of brown squares, which Matthew remembers his parents painting by hand "with very small paintbrushes."

Decorative additions include curtains, all secondhand, and an array of gorgeous lampshades, which Miranda makes to commission. Also made by her are the piles of fat cushions in glorious ikats and stripes, printed linens, and giant floral weaves, inviting you to slump on the deep sofas.

Slowly the house continues to evolve as furnishings come and go and rooms get the occasional revamp. A couple of years ago, they installed a roll-top bathtub in a back bedroom for the use of guests, and more recently they cleared out the old pantry between the living and dining rooms and made a laundry room far too beautiful to be wasted on washing, with a built-in hutch artfully dotted with old china. One day they may move, possibly abroad so Matthew can fulfill his long-term ambition to live somewhere hot, but Miranda says they will always keep a base in England. You can only hope that whoever buys their house won't paint over the smoke stains or strip the William Morris wallpaper.

ABOVE The bed in the main bedroom is a tall four-poster of faded glamour, made by Colefax and Fowler for Mr. and Mrs. Ronald Tree in the 1930s. Mrs. Tree, better known as her later incarnation Nancy Lancaster, was famously enamored of faded chintz. Miranda thinks the bed's curtains may be Victorian, as the pattern is so faint it has almost disappeared. The window curtains are also old chintz. Above the bedside table is an original E. H. Shepard cartoon given to Matthew and Miranda as a wedding present.

RIGHT One end of a spare bedroom has been curtained off to make a bathroom of elegant simplicity. The prints on either side of the 18th-century mirror are reproductions of the Rhinebeck Panorama, a four-sheet watercolor drawing of London dating from 1810.

ENGLISH ECCENTRIC
design elements

Eccentricity is not the sole preserve of the English. Other nations can boast many fine examples of extreme nonconformity, often coupled with brilliance; only think of Marcel Proust in his cork-lined room, Joseph Beuys with his coyote, or Ludwig of Bavaria and his fantasy palaces. But there is a particular type of eccentricity that seems peculiarly English: a mild, modest, even self-deprecating disregard for convention, which might be expressed by the transformation of a backyard into a miniature railroad, or dressing as Elvis Presley, or keeping a pig as a house pet. Mild eccentricity is invariably a delight to witness, particularly when expressed in the furnishing and decorating of a house. How much more exciting and intriguing it is to find yourself in rooms perfectly suited to the tastes, habits, and quirks of their inhabitants than surrounded by the bland, designerly trappings someone has seen in a magazine and slavishly copied in order to impress.

• COLOR The fashionable dominance of white paint is dwindling and color is making a comeback. Paint is the least expensive, most dramatic way of transforming a room. Raffaella Barker was inspired by a mixed bunch of garden flowers. You might find your inspiration hanging in your closet, or on a vegetable stand, or in Costa Rica or Pompeii. You can afford to be brave and original, since painting a room, if you do it yourself, costs time rather than money.

• FLOOR PAINT A floor of unattractive new or mismatched boards, ugly tiles, concrete, or hardboard is a good candidate for paint, whether a plain, all-over color as used by Raffaella Barker or a pattern of your own devising. Ordinary gloss or latex will wear off, but special floor paint is surprisingly durable.

• LATERAL THINKING Just because a room has always been a bedroom doesn't mean it couldn't be a kitchen. What about turning your walk-in pantry into a walk-in shower room? Both Raffaella Barker and Alan and Susanna Powers have used rooms in their houses in unconventional ways. You may not have the discipline to combine bedroom with library with dining room like the Powers, or the space to put a bath in a

bedroom like the Edens, but start "thinking out of the box" and you might find your rooms are more flexible than you thought.

• CLASHING PATTERN A healthy disregard for making things match can have surprisingly pleasing, if slightly unconventional, results, as in the Pruskins' living room.

• DO-IT-YOURSELF has got a bad name, but for true freedom of expression, you can't beat the homemade. It helps, of course, to have the eye of an artist as well as the skill of a craftsman, which doubtless accounts for the success of the Powers' bookcases and living-room curtains, and of the mural on the Edens' landing.

• COMMISSIONING If you have no faith in your own practical abilities, commissioning something custommade from an artist, or potter, or furniture maker can be a very satisfying and vicariously creative process. Raffaella Barker even chose the plates that Annabel Grey used to make the mosaic surround for her fireplace.

ISADORA'S HUT

ENGLISH ECCENTRIC finishing touches

Eccentric interiors are fascinating to look at, but impossible to be prescriptive about. The whole point of eccentricity is to defy categorization and evade the usual rules. In fact, if you have to try very hard to be eccentric, you will almost certainly succeed in being pretentious. The line between charming whimsy and irritating self-consciousness is a fine one, and simply putting a hat and pair of sunglasses on a fake classical bust as a gesture toward amusing originality will fall rather flat if the rest of the house is middle-of-the-road. That being said, wit is an important element of the eccentric interior. The "knocking back" of a very grand room or a rather pompous piece of furniture with something a little bit trashy or unexpected was one of Nancy Lancaster's tricks, and was equally espoused by John Fowler, who also recommended putting what he called an "ugly color" in a room to avoid prissy perfection.

• BOOKS There is nothing intrinsically eccentric about owning a lot of books, but they do seem to play a major role in some of the best eccentric interiors, which almost inevitably never have enough bookshelves to hold them. And so it is that books come to double as furnishings, with towers by the bed acting as overflow bedside tables, piles by the living-room couch as coffee tables, stacks used as doorstops, and even multiple stacks as makeshift room dividers.

• INCONGRUITIES The Powers have a Christmas-tree ornament hanging from their glamorous Regency mirror and a model dragon balancing on their living-room chandelier, while the Pruskins have a Victorian glass dome designed for a drawing-room mantelpiece on their kitchen sideboard. All are things strictly speaking in the wrong place, a fact that actually makes you appreciate them all the more.

• UNUSUAL USES Just as you can find new roles for rooms, so you can invent new and interesting uses for things. Raffaella Barker made her dining-room curtains out of mohair blankets. Alan Powers uses a large birdcage to house his stereo and flowerpots for flatware, while Matthew Eden keeps his coal in an antique fire extinguisher. The possibilities are endless.

• PERSONALIZE You may not be up to building a bookcase, but you can make something uniquely your own by adding to it, whether sticking a beaded edging around a lampshade or covering a shoebox with one of the Judd Street Gallery papers printed by the Powers.

• LEAVE WELL ENOUGH ALONE There is something disappointingly bland about an antique that has been over-restored. Mending old things that are shabby or broken is a subtle art. Go too far and you have lost all the romance of wear and tear and patina. Matthew Eden's treasured armchair, which appears on page 73, is a gorgeous example of just how chic shabby can be.

• THE HUNT Eccentricity is elusive and not readily found in the mall. Antique markets, secondhand stores, and bric-à-brac yard sales are far more fertile hunting grounds.

• KNOW WHAT YOU LIKE Whether your penchant is for wind-up toys or old garden tools, Victoriana or studio pottery, you can indulge it in your own home. Your passions may not be fashionable, but fashions change.

ENGLISH
ROSE

ACCORDING TO MEDIEVAL LEGEND, THE FIRST
ROSES, RED AND WHITE, BURST INTO BLOOM AT
THE FEET OF AN INNOCENT MAIDEN SENTENCED
TO BURN AT THE STAKE. LONG ASSOCIATED
WITH THE VIRGIN MARY, THE ROSE SYMBOLIZES
PURITY, BEAUTY, AND LOVE. A FADED ROSE
STANDS FOR TRANSIENCE, A WORM-EATEN ROSE
CORRUPTION, WHILE DOZENS OF VARIETIES
OF ROSE HAVE THEIR OWN MEANINGS. THE
ROSE IS ALSO THE EMBLEM OF ENGLAND,
OUR FAVORITE GARDEN PLANT, AND ONE
OF THE MOST ENDURING MOTIFS IN ENGLISH
DECORATION, AS SEEN IN THE FOLLOWING
FLOWER-FILLED HOUSES, WHERE IT APPEARS
ON EVERYTHING FROM WALLPAPER TO PLATES.

LEFT The kitchen is in the middle of the house, and has windows overlooking the outdoors on either side. At some stage in the 19th century, the older kitchen at the far end of the house was relegated to a laundry, and a new flue was built to house a cooking range where the 1940's Aga now stands. The chairs are Heal's, bought in Greenwich Market and dating from the early 20th century, and the pine table is also from Heal's, but a mere twenty years old. The original flagstones were moldering under several thick and sticky layers of vinyl flooring.

RIGHT The kitchen is freestanding. Plates and flatware are stored on top of an Arts and Crafts oak cupboard, mugs and glasses above.

TUDOR RESTORATION

ABOVE A Tudor gateway leads into the walled garden in front of the house. The house is in a small town, but has retained its gardens and a paddock. In the 17th century, the gardens reached the river, where the Duke of Monmouth reportedly "dallied" with a local girl.

This is my house. It must have seemed to anyone watching that we bought it on a whim. We lived and worked in London. We were not house-hunting. Our eldest daughter had just started at middle school. We viewed the house almost accidentally one half-term, and moved in two months later.

Of course there were practical considerations. It was conveniently close to an excellent school. It was in the middle of a small town and just around the corner from a store that was open on Sundays and after supper. It was also in countryside by the ocean, which I knew well from childhood. But more than this, it was old and utterly English, characteristics I find irresistibly attractive.

Pevsner thinks the house was once much bigger, but after four years of restoration, the discovery of a blocked-in fireplace, a Tudor privy, the remains of a spiral staircase, and a barrel-vaulted ceiling, we are not so sure. The local builder and stonemason who replaced the asbestos-tiled roof had a passion for early architecture and a practical knowledge born of more than fifty years' experience, and he couldn't figure out

LEFT The front of the house has a symmetrical façade and dates from the early 17th century, as does the fielded oak paneling in the living room. Although contemporary with the architecture of the room, the paneling does not fit properly and was probably moved from another room in the house in the 19th century. The painting by Arabella Johnson hangs over a sofa covered in natural linen. A large seagrass mat bound with dark brown leather covers the floorboards.

RIGHT In a corner of the same room is an Edwardian inlaid desk given as a wedding present. The 19th-century Venetian mirror was bought at auction and the leather chair from a gift shop in London. The brown velvet for the cushions on this chair and the sofas was originally curtains, pulled from a dumpster. To the right of the chair is a window, once a doorway, where a ghost is said to pass through. Opposite the second sofa, just seen on the left, is an enormous Tudor fireplace.

where another wing might have joined the existing building. The house is an architectural puzzle. Like most very old houses, it has been repeatedly altered. When first built it was the prestigious home of a family of rich Devon merchants. But it wasn't their only house, and by the end of the 17th century they had abandoned it completely in favor of homes more commodious and fashionable. For the next two hundred years, it was a working farmhouse.

Who knows at what point some pragmatic farmer decided that the forty-foot second-floor chamber with its high ceiling, large, drafty windows, and single fireplace would be better divided into three separate rooms, or when the old kitchen was relegated to laundry room and an old range installed where the Aga now sits? Mid-19th-century descriptions of the interior mention a richly carved staircase and elaborate "wainscotting"

upstairs and downstairs. Whatever the exact timing, by the 1920s most of these interior embellishments had gone in favor of something more plain and practical. Only one room is still paneled, but although the paneling is certainly 17th century, it has been installed in an untidy patchwork and was originally made for somewhere else.

Restoring the house has been a long process, some of it very dull, most of it very dusty. One of the most time-consuming tasks was chipping out and replacing with lime the slapped-on cement mortar that spread like a gray rash over the exterior stonework. It was a subtle transition aesthetically, but got rid of the damp. Other work was more exciting, like opening up the large second-floor chamber, reuniting its three matching windows, or removing the early 20th-century brickwork from Tudor fireplaces. Most of our alterations entailed removing

LEFT In our daughter Elizabeth's bedroom, the white metal four-poster is from The Iron Bed Company and is hung with cotton voile curtains.

RIGHT This room has always been known as the Monmouth Room in honor of the Duke of Monmouth, who is said to have stayed in the house on his royal progress through England before he became a pretender to the throne. Later, the owners put a plaque with the coat of arms and initials of King James above the fireplace here to prove their status as royalists. Shelves by local carpenter Peter Bennett fill one wall. The sofa is Regency and the 1940's table was from a local market.

things, whether partition walls or the compacted layers of linoleum that covered the flagstones on the kitchen floor. The greatest compliment is when a first-time visitor says that it looks as though we have done nothing at all to the house except furnish and decorate.

As Nancy Lancaster wisely advised, the first rule when decorating an old house is to "realize its period, feel its personality, and try to bring out its good points." There is a plain, no-nonsense feel about this house, with its thick flint and rubble walls and simple layout of two stout wings linked by a longer, central wing. There is also a pleasing generosity. The stone mullioned windows are tall and wide along the south front of the house, letting in plenty of sunlight, and the fireplaces are enormous in relation to the relatively modest rooms they were designed to heat.

Although this was once a house of high status, the way it is built on a natural slope —so that almost every downstairs room is on a different level, and every ceiling a different height—gives it a rambling,

informal feel. With its walled gardens of lawns and roses, it could only be English.

Without being slavish, Englishness became the decorative theme of the house. As it happened, most of the furnishings we brought with us fit the theme. A few pieces have been bought specially. The previous owner had a grandfather clock in the entrance hall, and the room seemed incomplete until we had found one to replace it, also made in Devon. The painting of a cow in a slice of Devon landscape is by a local artist, as is the photograph in negative of a christening dress from the collection at nearby Killerton. The wallpaper in our bedroom is Bowood from Colefax and Fowler, the very epitome of Englishness, and the curtains in the hall and the library are Bennison linens, which seem equally appropriate.

Although every generation that has lived in this house has changed something, no one has erased all traces of the past. The ancient arched wooden doorway to the old kitchen is patched like a well-worn pair of jeans and chewed at the edges but still

LEFT When the main part of the house was built in the mid-16th century, this second-floor room spanned the width of the central wing and had a barrel-vaulted ceiling and walls with molded plaster decoration, fragments of which can still be seen in the attic. In the early 20th century it was divided into three bedrooms and a long corridor. The corridor remains, but we took down the dividing walls so that the three large stone mullioned windows are now reunited in a single space to make a bedroom and bathroom. The wallpaper is Bowood from Colefax and Fowler, and the curtains are old linen sheets specially dyed by Polly Lyster.

ABOVE The room is partially divided by the Victorian flue from the kitchen below, against which we built fitted cupboards. The tub is a refurbished one, and a shower is tucked around the corner.

RIGHT Where possible we reused bathroom fixtures, like this roll-top bathtub in another bathroom. The wallpaper is from Canovas.

swings open on the iron brackets where it was first hung hundreds of years ago. The tiny leaded diamonds of glass in the downstairs powder room are pale green, striated and full of bubbles, cracked and buckled, engraved with names and an old motto, but no one has replaced them with new clear glass. We have added oak doors and built-in cupboards, but not much else that couldn't be taken away in a van. It sounds fanciful, but the house feels pleased with what we have done, and relieved by what we haven't.

LEFT A small front room leads straight into the kitchen, which Annabel has extended. Opposite the secondhand range, a door opens onto the steep wooden staircase. The kitchen units with their chic black granite tops were given to Annabel by a friend and were otherwise destined for a dumpster.

RIGHT The wall opposite the sink at the end of the kitchen is occupied by a hutch commissioned from a local craftsman to display Annabel's glorious collection of china, which includes Coalport and a swan teapot inherited from her grandmother, lots of luster teacups, and pink, yellow, and orange plastic salad bowls from T. K. Maxx. She treats its arrangement, she says, "like a painting." The spotted tablecloth is Annabel's own design.

ARTIST IN RESIDENCE

The first time Annabel Grey set foot inside her Norfolk cottage, she had to climb through a window, because the front door had not been opened for so long it was jammed shut. Tucked in the middle of a row of five Victorian farm cottages on a quiet village street, it had been empty since the death of its last occupant, a man who had lived in two of its four small rooms since he was born in one of them. There was no bathroom, a lean-to kitchen, and shared washhouses and privies at the back.

"It sounds rather romantic, but it was damp and derelict and completely uninhabitable," says Annabel. "But I was looking for a place I could escape to from my London flat, and here was something I could actually afford."

Although the house was tiny, there was enough land to put in a large shed that Annabel could use as a studio. Annabel works as a freelance designer, specializing in textiles, and often gets commissions for curtains and wall hangings, work that requires space. Fortunately, her new neighbors agreed to abolish the right of way along the back of the cottages

ABOVE The kitchen door opens onto a small paved terrace and a shed, once the old washhouse. A path leads between densely planted flowerbeds to Annabel's two studios. Annabel has worked as a florist, and in summer the house is full of gorgeous arrangements of flowers, mostly from her garden.

and to separate the yards with fencing. Annabel got part of a washhouse and a long patch of yard, which now houses two studio sheds. "I started to burst out of the first shed, so I gave up my parking space and put in another one."

Further collaboration with neighbors made it possible to extend the house at the back, doubling the size of the kitchen and adding a bathroom upstairs without losing the second bedroom. Two adjacent cottages were extended at the same time, and the work was done by the boyfriend of one of their owners. For two years Annabel visited and stayed with friends while her house was practically demolished and rebuilt. Old Norfolk pamments, square clay floor tiles, were unearthed in the front room, and one of the neighbors donated the old pamments from her own house so Annabel could continue the same flooring into the kitchen. A friend in London gave her the kitchen cabinets—complete with chic black granite counters—that were otherwise destined for a dumpster, and the bathtub was a builder's reject. Even the Rayburn was a secondhand bargain.

On a warm summer day, when the roses poke their pink heads through the white wooden porch and the kitchen door at the back opens into a tunnel of poppies, stocks, and delphiniums, the

LEFT When Annabel bought the cottage, there was no bathroom and the stairs led up to a tiny landing and two bedrooms. By extending at the back, she has made a landing and bathroom in the space of the original second bedroom, and a new second bedroom beyond. The patchwork quilt hanging over the stairs is Victorian.

OPPOSITE Shelves either side of the tiny Victorian fireplace hold ranks of Fulham Pottery vases, designed for flowers, but "so much nicer without them," as Annabel says, and each bought for no more than a few pounds. The painting is a self-portrait by Annabel's grandmother, the artist Margaret Kirkpatrick, whose uncle Frank Newberry was director of the Glasgow School of Art.

ABOVE The front door opens straight into the living room and onto Annabel's desk. To its left is a large squashy sofa and beyond it is the door into the kitchen. The floor is original pamments, square terracotta tiles often found in old Norfolk houses. A neighbor donated the pamments from her floors when she redecorated, enabling Annabel to continue the same flooring into the extended kitchen. The painting is *Nuclear Horse* by Jennifer Binney, and the floor lamp is 1950s.

cottage is as pretty as a fairytale. The tiny front room is half-filled by a huge sofa, draped in a hand-stitched quilt, and piled with pillows. The window has a Roman shade painted with colored spots the size of dinner plates, and the kitchen has a tablecloth in the same design. Pink and white china crams the kitchen hutch and, upstairs in the bathroom, a fringe of bead necklaces dangles from hooks along the edge of a shelf lined with glass vases, their round colored bases lined up like a selection of giant hard candy. All the walls and woodwork are painted white, but everywhere you look there is color and pattern. "Nothing has cost very much," says Annabel. "But I do spend hours arranging things. I think it's the textile designer in me—I treat the rooms as if they were paintings. If something doesn't fit, I can always sell it in my shop."

The shop, in the old stables at nearby Bayfield Hall, allows a process of continual turnover. Recent additions to the cottage interior include a pair of 1950's chairs upholstered in plastic-covered chintz and a large set of studio pottery that has already found its place, displayed on hooks and shelves above the kitchen door. Some things are sacrosanct, including the darkly handsome oil portrait of a Regency gentleman known as "the boyfriend," who gazes down upon Annabel's bed, and the paintings by her grandmother, the artist Margaret Kirkpatrick, from whom she also inherited some of her favorite china.

Annabel is a fan of her grandmother's paintings and her style. "She had Lucienne Day curtains and a nice, funny mix of antique furniture with more modern things. She loved color and always dressed beautifully. She even used to paint her shoes to match her outfits." Annabel seems to have inherited Margaret Kirkpatrick's tastes and talents, as well as some of her possessions and paintings.

RIGHT Running around the bathroom walls is a high shelf lined with single-stem vases from the 1950s and 1960s with solid glass bottoms in an array of translucent colors. They make a shiny, jewellike string of giant beads. Hanging below are some of Annabel's necklaces gathered on her travels, storage that is practical and pretty.

BELOW The bathroom, once part of the original second bedroom, lost its window when Annabel extended the cottage, so is now lit by a skylight. It has a solid, old-fashioned feel with an extra-large tub, bought cheaply as a second, and white brick-shaped tiling.

THIS PICTURE AND LEFT
The spare bedroom occupies the space above the kitchen extension and has a sloping roof and a dormer window overlooking the yard. Opposite the old iron bedstead are deep built-in cupboards, which help to make up for the lack of attic storage. A high shelf holds books, its brackets copied from those supporting the Victorian mantelpiece downstairs. More books are stacked at the end of the bed.

ABOVE LEFT The imposing front door of the house, with its classical relieving arch and molded stone surround, was obviously designed to impress visitors. It opens into an equally imposing entrance hall with a stone floor and a stone staircase sweeping up to a wide landing behind a rather grandiose pair of pillars.

ABOVE RIGHT Everything about the entrance to this house speaks of prosperity. In the days before street lighting, the lantern above the gate would have provided illumination up the steps to the front door.

LEFT The living room, with its high ceiling and tall sash windows, was added at the beginning of the 19th century. Elizabeth has painted the walls a soft terracotta pink because she finds it such a welcoming color. The chintz curtains are antique, their plain pink borders added by Elizabeth to fit the windows in her last house. The Victorian sofa is upholstered in old silk velvet and needlepoint.

PRESERVING THE FABRIC

Bradford-on-Avon in Wiltshire is like a miniature, slightly rustic, Bath. Built on the proceeds of the wool trade, its houses date back to the 15th century and earlier. But its most imposing façades are Georgian—smooth-faced, double-fronted, symmetrical. The façade of Elizabeth and Derek Baer's house is particularly impressive, with a central pediment over an elaborately pilastered Venetian window.

The weighty paneled front door opens into an equally splendid hall, its wide stone staircase rising behind a pair of hefty columns. "It's all show," laughs Elizabeth Baer. "When the house was first built in about 1730, it was grafted onto some much earlier weavers' cottages. It's really one room deep with some funny-shaped rooms behind—what remains of the cottages. The façade and the hall are by far the grandest things about it."

LEFT Open fires are a focus in all three reception rooms and add to the sense of comfort and welcome in the living room. The charmingly battered armchairs with original upholstery look particularly inviting. Above the fire hangs a framed embroidery sewn by the oldest daughter of King Louis XV of France and her ladies-in-waiting as an altar frontal.

RIGHT The dining room leads off to the right from the hall and retains its original early 18th-century paneling. Although the room is quite small, it has an elaborately molded plaster ceiling, also original. The intimate round table and the fact that the room leads into the living room make it feel cozy and lived in, even though it is not often used for dining.

On either side of the ostentatious entrance are two reception rooms. What they lack in floor space they make up for with some particularly fine architectural embellishments: an exceptional carved wooden chimney piece in the living room on the left, featuring plump roses so perfectly three-dimensional you could pick them; and in the dining room original paneling and a gorgeously molded plaster ceiling. Upstairs there are two bedrooms above each of these rooms and a further two on the third floor. The kitchen and bathrooms fill the "funny-shaped rooms" behind. In the 1820s a three-story extension was added to the right-hand side of the house to make a fashionably high-ceilinged living room, which leads from the dining room, and more bedrooms above. Before that, this splendid façade fronted nothing much more fancy than a two-up, two-further-up, and two-down house.

The result of grand classical ideas applied to such a small plot is a building of typically English quirkiness. As with so many old houses, it is the architectural discrepancies, the surprises and changes of scale, which give it its charm. Elizabeth and Derek have nurtured and restored some of the original features,

chipping cement from the stone stairs and replacing the missing pieces of carving on the living-room chimney piece. This kind of careful restoration is not cheap, but Elizabeth claims to have furnished and decorated "on a shoestring."

If you didn't happen to know better, you might not believe her. But Elizabeth Baer is mistress of the make-do-and-mend school of interior decoration. She deals in antique textiles and can claim to have invented the fashion for using old French linen sheets as curtains and upholstery. Her passion for textiles was ignited many years ago when she bought two chinoiserie quilts from antique dealer Robin Eden, whose son Matthew's house is also featured in this book (see pages 68–75). Some years later, on a buying trip to France, a dealer pressed on her some antique sheets because she said they were such good value. Elizabeth hung one at a window as a temporary measure while waiting to have proper curtains made. But it attracted such comment and admiration that she made it into curtains. And so began a thriving business, its success founded on an aesthetic arbitrage between the English love of the old and faded, and the widespread French disdain for it.

It was also Elizabeth Baer who discovered the delights of French ticking, striped in gorgeous colors and tight-woven as featherproof covering for old-fashioned mattresses. She first came across them in a barn where the feathers were being stripped out for reuse in skiwear and the covers recycled as rag. Once they were washed and ironed, it was instantly obvious how desirable this fabric was for cushions and upholstery. She sold every scrap and went back for more, several times.

Nearly fifteen years later, old French ticking is an expensive rarity. Fortunately the supply of sheets is more plentiful, as yet more chests and armoires are steadily emptied of their contents. The basement of the house is lined with racks of linen, all laundered,

LEFT To the left of the entrance hall, opposite the dining room, is a cozy sitting room with windows on two sides and an 18th-century wooden chimney piece charmingly carved with roses. The fabrics, including curtains and pillow covers, are secondhand.

FAR LEFT The kitchen, behind the formal front rooms, occupies the space where there was once a row of medieval weavers' cottages. The main part of the house was built onto these cottages in the 18th century, and the rooms at the back of the house, in contrast with the classical symmetry of the rooms at the front, have walls at odd angles and a much older feel.

CENTER AND LEFT One of the front second-floor bedrooms is a showroom for some of the fine antique fabrics which Elizabeth Baer buys and sells. Much of her stock comes from France, turned out from the capacious linen cupboards of châteaux and *maisons de ville*. Smaller items are displayed on the shelves of her own old English linen cupboard.

The stairs, hall, and landing, perhaps the only parts of the house seen by many visitors, were designed to be impressive, with elaborate barley-twist banisters complementing wide stone steps and a large Venetian window flooding light onto the landing. Antique curtains for sale are displayed on short lengths of rail on the wall. The sofa is covered with antique French ticking.

LEFT AND ABOVE The main bedroom is predominantly pink, like the living room. When the house was used as a bank in the 19th century, this room was an office. The door on the left of the fireplace leads to the bathroom and a small strongroom where the money was stored, and which now houses Elizabeth's shoes. The four-poster bed is dressed with an antique toile de Jouy scalloped valance and antique quilt. A Victorian tambour lace bedspread is stretched across the canopy and secured with thumbtacks.

sorted and labeled, and ready to be reinvented at the windows and on the chairs and sofas of chic interiors. The fashion for heavily textured cloth, such as the rough hemp sheets used in poorer homes, has widened the market to include old grain sacks and cow and horse blankets, which are often charmingly cross-stitched with the initials of their owners. While sheets are stored in the basement, a pretty second-floor bedroom is a showroom for Elizabeth's stock of fine linens, toiles de Jouy, damask napkins, lace, embroidery, and antique curtains.

Needless to say, every curtain, bedspread, bed hanging, cushion, and upholstery fabric in the house has had another life elsewhere, often adjusted to suit its new circumstances by Elizabeth herself. The drawing-room curtains are Victorian chintz. Elizabeth added wide borders of plain pink cotton to make them fit the Georgian windows of her last house. Not only did they also fit the four windows of her new living room perfectly, but there were just the right number. The dining room has curtains in an early 20th-century tree-of-life design. There were three: two frame the window and the third was cut up to make a ruffled valance and a hanging on the wall opposite. Upstairs, Elizabeth's charming four-poster bed has a canopy made from a Victorian tambour lace bedspread. "The net stretches beautifully," smiles Elizabeth with satisfaction, "so you can make it fit very snugly."

These old fabrics, combined with Elizabeth and Derek's collection of antique furniture, most bought before it became unaffordable, give the house a slightly faded grandeur and create the illusion that they have lived here all their lives, instead of a mere three years.

LEFT In the spare bedroom at the top of the house the colors are soft muted blues and greens, based around the faded paintwork of the French wood and cane bedsteads. As in all the rooms, the curtains, bedspreads, and quilts are antique. Although Elizabeth and Derek have only recently finished decorating the house, the soft, worn quality of the fabrics makes every room feel comfortably broken in, as though they have lived here for decades.

MATERIAL WEALTH

The Norfolk rectory owned by Gilly and Geoff Newberry is the sort of small English country house that every reluctant city dweller dreams of. Opposite the ancient flint church, but hidden from the road by a screen of mature trees, it is Georgian, red brick, a child's drawing with a door in the middle and windows on either side. It faces lawn sliding into the longer grass of a meadow through which a wide mown path wends its curvy way toward a wooden gate and a view framed by a canopy of leaves across fields toward woodland.

ABOVE The house is approached up a long drive to the back courtyard, where the architecture is more cottagey and asymmetrical as a result of extensions. The front retains its classical symmetry. Wide mown paths lead from the front door to the lane and fields beyond.

LEFT Bennison recently introduced a line of wallpapers based on archive prints, but many of the rooms in the house have fabric stretched on battens providing pattern for the walls—here, Pondicherry in a spare bedroom.

Beyond the symmetry of the façade, the house spreads comfortably. To the left it extends in a long wing containing the kitchen, to the right it reaches back to the lean-to garden room with its sloping glazed roof and French doors overlooking a deep herbaceous border. There are roses clambering across the front of the house and a huge wisteria reaching up and around the side. There are clipped yew trees, a cobbled courtyard, urns, and a pond.

Inside, the English idyll continues, reinforced by the faded floral fabrics that cover plump sofas and their fat cushions, hang at the windows upstairs and

BELOW The far end of the kitchen is an extension, designed by Geoff Newberry with a clean, modern feel. The room is big enough to accommodate two large oak tables, also designed by Geoff, one of which sits behind the sofa, the other at right angles to it out of the picture to provide an extra work surface at the business end of the room. The floor is reclaimed terracotta tiles, and the French doors overlook a terrace and a small pond.

stretch across bedroom walls like soft wallpaper. This is chintz at its most sophisticated: traditional designs printed in subtle colors on earthy linen.

In the pretty living room Gilly has just had the sofas and armchairs recovered in fresh indigo resist linen, its intense blue a perfect match for the old Delft tiles that line the fireplace. In another house this could be construed as extravagance, since the previous rose-strewn upholstery was barely worn. But, as owner of the company that sells the fabrics, Gilly has motives more businesslike than a simple desire for novelty. "I like to try our new designs out," Gilly explains. "I have always used this house as a kind of showcase. It suits the fabrics so perfectly."

In 1985 Gilly established Bennison Fabrics, reproducing patterns from 18th- and 19th-century originals and expanding on the line of document fabrics created by the antique dealer and decorator Geoffrey Bennison. Having worked as his assistant, Gilly developed a passion for antique textiles, which she collects and sometimes uses to add to the line.

Gilly says she owes Geoffrey Bennison far more than the legacy of his name and his cupboards full of old fabrics. "He was the most enormous influence on my taste, and the taste of many others," she says. "His interiors had a richness and grandeur, but they

LEFT AND ABOVE RIGHT The living room has a window onto the front yard and a bay window fringed with wisteria overlooking the clipped yew and herbaceous border at the side of the house. The deep, generously cushioned chairs and sofas have been upholstered in Bennison's new line of indigo resist fabrics, which happen to be a perfect match for the 17th-century Delft tiles that surround the fireplace. The 18th-century portrait of the Werz family above the sofa once belonged to Geoffrey Bennison.

RIGHT The morning room across the hall from the kitchen is papered in one of Bennison's new line of wallpapers.

were always comfortable and, even when newly decorated, they felt lived in. He had a fantastic sense of scale and often used very large pieces in small spaces and, of course, he loved old and faded fabrics."

Geoffrey Bennison's taste pervades Gilly's house, and some of his possessions decorate it. The blue-and-white china meat plates that hang on the walls of the corridor between the kitchen and morning room once belonged to him, as did the life-size 18th-century family portrait in the living room. The arrangement of the lavishly draped four-poster bed in the main bedroom, with its attendant pair of Corinthian column pot cupboards and alabaster lamps, is a faithful copy of the furnishings in Bennison's own bedroom—"my homage," as Gilly calls it.

There is another Geoffrey in Gilly Newberry's life who should take equal credit. Her husband and business partner, also a designer, has a "vision" which Gilly claims to lack. Geoff Newberry designed the new garden room with its round window the size of a cart wheel, and insisted on the four-foot-high blue-and-white pot lamps, which Gilly thought would be too big for the space, but which Geoffrey Bennison would surely have championed, too. He also designed the extension to the original kitchen and the matching oak tables that furnish it. The house combines Geoff's eye for proportion and scale with Gilly's love of fabrics, and a generous dash of Bennison thrown in. It's a good recipe.

ABOVE LEFT The main bedroom with its heavily draped four-poster and walls lined with flowery fabric is Gilly's "homage" to Geoffrey Bennison. The 18th-century appliquéd bedspread is used sparingly to prevent wear.

BELOW LEFT The master bathroom boasts a bathtub to match the splendor of the bedroom, an Edwardian feat of plumbing incorporating an early "walk-in" shower complete with extra-large shower head and jets of water from all directions. The fabric-covered walls complete the sense of luxury.

ABOVE The garden room, another of Geoff's "visions," is a great success, its wall of windows and glass doors affording a fine view of the lawns and herbaceous border. The giant lamps, converted from antique pots, are the kind of over-scaled decorative items Geoffrey Bennison might have used.

RIGHT Gilly and Geoff's daughter's bedroom is a feast of fat, faded roses, again with fabric lining the walls. With curtains and valances in the same fabric, a flower-strewn quilt and rosebud-scattered pillows, you can almost smell a summer garden and hear the buzz of bees—even in winter.

ENGLISH ROSE design elements

The English love affair with the garden has been a long and faithful one. Look out of the window of a train as you rumble across England through villages, towns, suburbs, even cities, and you will see patches of lawn, paved terraces, shrubs, apple trees, rows of lettuce, each house with an attached bib or collar of green, a little slice of countryside all of its own. The importance of a garden to the English is deeper than a simple love of flowers and grass. More than a means of expression, an Englishman's house is his territory, his castle, and to have some enclosed space surrounding it, at front and back or ideally all around, is to have a buffer between the private life of home and the public one beyond. Certainly the blurring of boundaries between indoor and outdoor space with conservatories and garden rooms, or French doors leading onto fully furnished terraces, is a characteristic of English domestic design. And such is our devotion that we find a hundred ways of bringing our love of horticulture indoors, from cultivating house plants and filling vases with fresh flowers to covering walls, chairs, curtains, cushions, and china with flowery, leafy pattern.

• FABRICS are the most obvious way to introduce flowers to a decorative scheme. There is a vast herbaceous border of new flower-strewn fabrics to choose from, ranging from the contemporary and stylized to the traditional, from very expensive embroidered silks to cheap and jolly printed cottons.

• PATTERN AND PLAIN After more than a decade of plain walls and plain fabrics as the dominant fashion for interiors, too much pattern can still seem visually indigestible. Balance areas of pattern with plenty of plain—flowery cushions on a plain sofa, sprigged curtains against painted walls—for a fresh, pretty effect.

• MIXING PATTERNS Checks, stripes, and sprigs work particularly well with flowery designs. Late 18th- and early 19th-century French toile de Jouy bed hangings were lined with "Vichy" fabric, an extra-large check of pinkish-red or indigo blue and white, the deep valances scalloped and quilted. English chintz bed hangings were often contrasted with a lining in a small sprigged pattern, picking up one of the colors of the chintz. These pleasing pairings of large, loose patterns with the straight lines of checks and stripes, or the small, neat grid of a sprig, can be used in all kinds of ways, from curtains and cushions to upholstery.

• WALLPAPER Along with the demise of all-white walls has come a revival of wallpaper, much of it bolder and more theatrical than ever, and another way of garlanding your house with flowers and foliage. Smaller patterns like sprigs or posies are easier to live with than big designs with big repeats. If you don't want to be enveloped by it, you can always use wallpaper on one wall only.

• FURNITURE The pretty, painted Regency furniture featuring delicate wreaths and medallions of flowers and foliage that was so often a key element in John Fowler's decorating schemes is now prohibitively expensive. Imitating it successfully is a rare skill, but you can capture some of its elegance and femininity by painting a well-chosen chair, for example, a pale color and padding its seat in a flowery fabric.

ENGLISH ROSE finishing touches

Turning raw nature into tamed pattern is one of the many ways we appreciate the beauty of the natural world, and is far from exclusively English. Nevertheless, what we now think of as the archetypal English interior, whether a cottage with geraniums on the windowsill and rosebuds on the teapot, or a rectory living room with peonies on the grand piano and posies on the curtains, is characterized by its predominantly floral decoration and a preponderance of flower-related ornaments. As John Cornforth said of the charming, chintzy rooms created by John Fowler, "even in London he seems able to suggest bees buzzing among roses," which, fresh from a dusty pavement after a long day in an air-conditioned office, is rather a lovely thought.

• FRESH FLOWERS When asked to reveal her "decorating secrets," Nancy Lancaster always said she had only three, and that they were "open fires, candlelight, and flowers." Flowers need not be expensive, but they must be fresh. A huge vase of cow parsley changed every day, a mound of primroses in a mug, or a single garden rose in a glass bottle are much lovelier than drooping hothouse flowers in slimy water.

• POTTED PLANTS tend to conjure images of dusty leaves on office windowsills but, well chosen and well tended, last much longer than cut flowers and can provide scent and indoor greenery all year round. Hydrangeas, miniature roses, stephanotis, jasmine, and geraniums are all good choices. Place ugly plastic pots inside terracotta flowerpots and cluster smaller pots together, perhaps in a lined basket, or line them up in a row for more impact.

• QUILTS Quilted feather eiderdowns were turned out by the ton in the first half of the last century, judging by how many are to be found for sale in antique and secondhand shops. They are often covered in delightful vintage floral fabric, are no more expensive than a decent duvet, and can be laid on top

of a bed for instant, old-fashioned charm. Do be sure to give them a good shake before you buy, as some shed feathers like confetti.

• CHINA Handpainted 18th- or 19th-century china, decorated with flowers, is as pleasurable to use as it is to look at and, if you don't mind the odd chip, crack, or rivet, very affordable. Crammed on a hutch, as in Annabel Grey's kitchen, or neatly posed on a mantelpiece, it is wonderfully decorative. Make up a teaset from odd cups, saucers, and plates, lay out a cloth, and cut some dainty sandwiches. But don't put the dishes in the dishwasher afterward.

• PICTURES In the first half of the 19th century, an essential skill taught to young ladies of leisure was painting in watercolors, and a favorite subject was flowers. These watercolors, which typically filled leather-bound albums, have great delicacy and charm and, being relatively numerous and amateur, are not expensive. Old botanical prints, close-hung and identically framed, have a graphic appeal.

ENGLISH COUNTRY HOUSE

THE ENGLISH COUNTRY HOUSE HAS LENT ITS NAME TO A STYLE OF INTERIOR DECORATION THAT HAS NEVER BEEN ENTIRELY OUT OF FASHION SINCE IT CRYSTALLIZED MORE THAN HALF A CENTURY AGO. ODDLY, IT TOOK AN AMERICAN HEIRESS, IN PARTNERSHIP WITH THE ENGLISH SON OF A RACECOURSE CLERK, TO INVENT AND PERFECT IT. NANCY LANCASTER AND JOHN FOWLER'S TALENTS COMBINED TO CREATE INTERIORS THAT WERE ELEGANTLY INFORMAL, HISTORICALLY SENSITIVE, AND SUPREMELY COMFORTABLE. TODAY'S VERSION OF THE STYLE MAY HAVE DITCHED THE RUFFLES, PAINT EFFECTS, AND PICTURES HUNG FROM BOWS, BUT THE ESSENTIALS ARE UNCHANGED.

REVIVING THE PAST

The oldest wing of Columbine Hall rises from the undulating Suffolk countryside like a crooked galleon. This ancient, jettied, timber structure, still protected on two sides by its original moat, was built as the service wing to a late 14th-century great hall, which stood opposite and has long been demolished. Today it forms the longest leg of a U-shaped house built around a central courtyard.

ABOVE The long gabled wing on the left is the oldest part of the house, its original timber frame masked by later decorative plaster known as pargetting. The newest part of the house is the wing on the far right, added in the 1840s and housing the drawing room.

LEFT Leslie Geddes-Brown writes about gardens, interior design, and food and, although old-fashioned in feel, her kitchen is well equipped. The central work surface is an old butcher's block—ideal for food preparation.

ABOVE RIGHT The Victorian pine cupboards have been extended across the wall and up to follow the eccentric slope of the ceiling, an angle mirrored by the floor of the main bedroom above. Shelving behind the paneled doors houses Leslie's huge collection of cookbooks, plus jars of spices and sauces. The room was originally a kitchen and a scullery. Installing a new floor of antique terracotta tiles helped to give the impression that this was always a single space.

RIGHT Leslie kept the old range from the original kitchen, still run on solid fuel, hence the coal scuttles. Skillets, saucepans, and a colander hang from hooks, an arrangement which not only looks picturesque but is practical.

The house is home to writer Leslie Geddes-Brown and her husband Hew Stevenson. When first built, Columbine Hall was fit for a nobleman, but by the 18th century it had the status of a farmhouse and was rented, then sold to farmers. In 1993 the last family to live there decided to sell.

Today Columbine Hall is cradled in the midst of gardens and fields, but fifteen years ago it was swamped by ugly barns, towering silos, rusting machinery, and all the other indistinguishable detritus of a working farm. "We always play a game after we visit a new house," says Leslie, "which is to plan what we would do with it if we were forced to own it. By the time we got back to London, we desperately wanted to buy this house."

Hew and Leslie's sealed bid was successful, and in 1993 they took possession and set about stripping this ancient manor house back to its essential beauty. Recent farm buildings were demolished. The base of one became the low brick wall around a vegetable garden, the only early barn was scrubbed up as a beamed and vaulted venue for parties, and the old gig house was converted, making a charming vacation cottage. George Carter (see pages 168–75) helped with the design of these buildings and their surrounding gardens, and Melvyn Smith was responsible for many of their architectural embellishments and for the restoration of the main house.

Melvyn Smith was a canny choice. Leslie had first come across him when

RIGHT The dining room on the ground floor of the 14th-century wing of the house overlooks the moat on two sides and is constantly bathed in the gentle flicker of light reflected in water. Beneath the rush matting is a brick floor found under a later layer of concrete. Furnishings, including a 17th-century oak table and 18th-century Windsor chairs, plain linen curtains, and a set of prints of kings and queens of England, have a simple, robust quality, reminiscent of 17th-century Dutch interiors.

BELOW LEFT The central reception room, which faces the front door, is known as the Moat Room. An East European painted settle piled with blue and white cushions, and a 17th-century painting of Baden Baden spa, make a grouping that again remind one of early Dutch interiors.

BELOW The wide brick medieval fireplace in the dining room, like the brick floor, was hidden by later additions. In this room an early ceiling was also discovered, still intact above the lower lath and plaster ceiling.

she worked for *The World of Interiors* magazine, in which his own house was featured. Trained as an engineer but with a passion for old buildings, Melvyn had created his own paneled, shuttered, flagstoned, and porticoed manor house from a derelict shell in Derbyshire that had lost all its architectural features. Columbine Hall was a very different proposition, as it was in sound condition and bristling with period detail. "I knew Melvyn could do whatever work was necessary, but also that he would appreciate the building deeply enough not to peel away its character," Leslie explains.

In the event, Melvyn exceeded his brief and added more character on top. Without the benefit of Leslie and Hew's enthusiastic candor, you would assume that they had moved into Columbine Hall having done nothing more than give the house a good scrub with lukewarm water and old-fashioned soap flakes. In fact, the interior today results from a judicious combination of the undoing of later work, leaving well enough alone, and some extremely convincing fakery.

Careful excavation revealed unexpected additional features. In the dining room alone, Melvyn found the brick floor preserved under a layer of concrete, the wide medieval fireplace, which had been blocked in, and the original beamed ceiling with its dirty gray patina still intact above a later layer of lath and plaster. Clever to find them; even more clever not to attempt to seal the brick floor or paint the ceiling, so the room simply seems to have mellowed with use over the centuries.

So far, so original, but next door in the kitchen all is not quite as ancient as it looks. Here a wall was removed to make a larger room and original Victorian cupboards seamlessly modified and expanded. The blue limewash paint, which is flaking in a picturesque if unintentional

ABOVE The winding oak Jacobean staircase has been in place for a long time, but was almost certainly taken from another house, architectural salvage being a rather older practice than one might suspect. The map, dated 1741, was made for Ambrose Crowley when he inherited large estates. This shows all his land and property, including Columbine Hall, which squeezes in as "an also-ran on the bottom right," as Leslie puts it.

FAR LEFT The drawing room, added to the house in the 1840s, is a triumph of fakery with plywood paneling constructed by Melvyn Smith in early 18th-century style and incorporating an 18th-century Italian landscape painting. Furnishings are defiantly not in period and include a 1920's sofa and armchair in cut moquette, bought "for a pittance," and three Chinese tables.

LEFT Another downstairs room with fake paneling is known as William's Room after a cousin of Hew's who stayed there to do the garden. The chairs are 18th-century English, painted white, and the lamp and shade come from Ducci in Florence.

RIGHT In a spare room the wooden bedstead is made from collapsed 17th-century chests. The blocked-in window above the bed is medieval, and the room also features a fragment of medieval wall painting. It is known as the Poley Room after Sir John Poley, a 17th-century owner of the house.

BELOW Melvyn Smith made the paneling in this bathroom and did the drawing of Columbine Hall.

FAR RIGHT The timber frame of the medieval wing can be clearly seen in these upstairs rooms, the walls and floors of which have warped and bent over the centuries. After repeatedly rolling out of bed due to the pronounced slope of the floor, Hew and Leslie commissioned a new bed with legs on one side longer than on the other, assuring a level mattress. The brass-studded trunk at the foot of the bed is 18th century.

manner, was copied from the kitchens at Calke Abbey (blue was traditionally used in kitchens, as it was thought to repel flies) and adds to the sense that this room has hardly changed for generations. The lovely dark gray and fox-brown tiled floor is old, but new to Columbine Hall.

The boldest pseudo-historical creation is the drawing room, which forms part of the wing added opposite the medieval one in the 1840s. Thanks to Melvyn, the room now feels at least a century older, wrapped in paneling of early 18th-century design. Somehow Melvyn has bashed

and battered and even slightly cracked the plywood, so that it has the genuine feel of having survived a couple of hundred years of hot fires and cold winters. It even hides the radiators.

It should be no surprise, then, to discover that the library is also an example of Melvyn's woodwork or that he made the venerable-looking curved metal shower at the end of a bathtub, or the paneling with integral desk and drawers in the little downstairs room known as William's Room in honor of a guest.

It almost seems greedy to have added more history to a house already reeking with it, but perhaps it is irresistible when you have employed someone so good at doing it. In any house occupied for many generations, there are relics of the tastes and habits of the past. Hew and Leslie have not only preserved and rediscovered some of these; they have added their own, plus very discreet heating, plumbing, and wiring. "We have a house in Tuscany which we have done a lot of work on," says Leslie. "Our Italian builder Maurizio finds it very amusing that we don't want everything straightened and tidied up, which he says is typical of the English."

ELIZABETHAN JEWEL

Simon Johnson describes the process of restoring and decorating his house on the edge of a tiny Somerset village as an exercise in "paring away the layers." The oldest portion of the house, now the dining room and living room, dates back some six hundred years. In the 16th century this relatively humble single-story building was ostentatiously extended at one end with a three-story flourish of gables and soaring chimneys, containing a sizeable room on each floor and incorporating the grand gesture of a wide wooden staircase winding up in its own stone tower. The effect must have been disconcertingly lopsided until in the 17th century a second story was added to the original part of the house.

ABOVE The earliest part of the house is the ground floor on the left. The three-story addition on the right with its soaring chimneys contains the staircase and the living room, and dates from the 16th century.

LEFT A later wing at the back of the house was being used as a storeroom when the Johnsons moved in. By knocking down a wall, they extended the small working kitchen into this space. They also added an internal door leading to the room beyond, now a scullery, which had been a stable box accessible only from outside. The table and chairs are modern pine, painted dark navy blue, now attractively worn and chipped. The heavily carved cupboard to the right of the door is a pair of chests from Afghanistan, one on top of the other and modified to house a television and stereo.

RIGHT The painted tile mural above the Aga range is a portrait of the house and family, and was commissioned from ceramic artist Penny Green, who also made the plates above.

In the 19th century the house spread a little farther, with a single story jutting out at right angles into the garden at the back. Twentieth-century accretions included concrete and linoleum over original flagstones and a fake stone fireplace.

"The house today bears precious little resemblance to the house we bought," says Simon. "In fact, I would say we had to replace about sixty percent. The roof was crumbling, there was dry rot, and some of the beams were so soft you could literally scoop them out with a spoon." Unpicking the house back to its bare bones and rebuilding what had decayed beyond repair became a full-time career for Simon, who put his work as a garden designer on hold to manage a team of builders and spent his days mixing mortar, carrying bricks, and recycling roof slates while his wife Antonia devoted herself to childcare. "We moved in a week after our eldest daughter, Maudie, was born and lived in two rooms. By the time our second child, Edmund, was born fifteen months later, it was better, and quite civilized when we had Beatrice."

LEFT In the inner hall are two pieces inherited by Antonia Johnson: a heavily carved 17th-century Italian chest on a later base, and hanging over it an 18th-century mahogany and gilt mirror that belonged to her grandmother. Looking through into the dining room, the picture is by Israeli artist Amikam Toren.

LEFT AND BELOW LEFT The dining room is in the oldest part of the house and retains its enormous blue lias flagstones, preserved under layers of linoleum and painstakingly cleaned on hands and knees by Simon Johnson as part of the restoration. The ladder-back chairs were made for them by Robert Kime, who also supplied the Arts and Crafts table with its bleached and scrubbed top. The oil painting over the table is by stained-glass artist Thomas Denny, while the picture on the left is by Scottie Wilson.

RIGHT The Johnsons put in the Victorian register grate and plain surround in the living room to replace an ugly 20th-century fireplace. Above it hangs a painting by Edward Burra called *Revolver Dream*, bought by Antonia twenty years ago in partial exchange for another 20th-century work. The large padded stool is covered in a kilim bought in a flea market in Hungary.

The house today represents what Simon calls a "comfortable equilibrium." "We stripped the house right back, to bare plaster, bare boards, and original fireplaces, to find its inherent beauty and then, if the effect was too spartan and empty, we added something." One of their more ambitious additions was the plasterwork in the drawing room. This is the ground-floor chamber of the grand Elizabethan extension and the scene of a particularly exciting moment in the restoration, when the original Tudor chimney piece was found languishing behind a 1950's fireplace. "We added the stone lintel, which we copied from one at Muchelney Abbey, and we took

our inspiration for the plaster frieze from a bigger house of the same date nearby. It was sculpted by Eve Body using 16th-century techniques, and we chose as motifs all the creatures that are helpful to gardeners, so there are ladybugs and butterflies, beetles and bumblebees." The effect is charming and entirely in tune with the original date of the room.

The way the house is furnished represents another equilibrium, in this instance between the differing tastes of Simon and Antonia. "I like more modernity than Simon," explains Antonia, who worked in the field of contemporary art before training at the English Gardening School. Fortunately for marital harmony, the robust simplicity of the architecture, with its bare floorboards, gently undulating plaster, and stone mullioned windows, is well suited to both their tastes.

With admirable lack of sentiment, they sold the family heirlooms that did not suit this aesthetic—"all the Georgian

LEFT The Tudor stone fireplace in the drawing room was hidden behind 1950's fake stone. The Johnsons added a stone lintel copied from one at nearby Muchelney Abbey. The plasterwork above it and the frieze are also new, designed by Eve Body. The pair of crested chairs is from the coronation of King George VI, used on the occasion by Antonia's grandparents.

RIGHT The painted paneling and paneled closet in the main bedroom were made by Stuart Interiors with a carved frieze copied from stonework on the exterior of the house. The antique Bible box and carved chest were also bought from Stuart Interiors, and the painting above is *Lovers, Faces, and Cliffs* by Ken Kiff.

BELOW A view from the landing into a bathroom made by Ken Bell, the builder responsible for much of the interior detail in the house. The basin is set in a Victorian washstand.

mahogany," as Simon puts it. When funds allowed, they bought early pieces such as the huge 17th-century tapestry in the staircase hall from decorator Robert Kime, and the Italian *cassone* (chest) beneath it. More economic buys were the old Indian *suat* chests, which are as chunky and heavily carved as Jacobean furnishings but fortunately cheap enough to justify modification. The one in the kitchen now houses the television and stereo. Modernity is confined to the walls, a couple of large oil landscapes, and in the dining room abstract photographic images of flowers and seed heads by Karl Blossfeldt. Some things make an elegant leap between the centuries: a piece of 16th-century needlework from antique dealer Christopher Gibbs in the drawing room has the graphic beauty of a contemporary artwork, as do the Native American parfleche pouches, folded like origami and decorated with linear, symbolic designs.

After twenty years working on prestigious commissions on both sides of the Atlantic, Simon makes a ready link between the English styles of gardening and of interior design. "In both cases," he says, "it's partly having the confidence to leave things as they are, but it's also having the eye to put together things from all over the place—statuary, plants, furniture—and make something harmonious."

LEFT Endsleigh is that architectural oddity, a house designed to look smaller and more humble than it really is, with a cottage exterior of steep gables and leaded lights masking the space and comfort of a Regency aristocrat's home. The veranda, supported by rough tree trunks and paved with knobbly sheep's knuckles, affords a ravishing view across a steep, wooded valley of the River Tamar.

A STATELY COTTAGE

English country-house style at its grandest and most traditional was the product of a way of life that was the privilege of aristocrats and the landed gentry, and which had dissolved by the middle of the last century. No one can emulate this lifestyle today. It isn't just that it would be prohibitively expensive, or impractical; it would simply feel uncomfortable in our more egalitarian society. The closest we can come to experiencing the daily life of history's megarich is to stay in a country-house hotel. One of the best is Endsleigh.

LEFT The capacious entrance hall with its dark paneling and baronial fireplace instantly announces that this is no ordinary country cottage. Olga Polizzi has furnished the room simply and sparsely, and although the vase of flowers on the central table is magnificent in scale, the flowers are locally picked ferns, foxgloves, and oak leaves. For most of the year there is a fire blazing in the grate, and guests arriving after dark are greeted by the magical sight of dozens of purple glass votives set around the edge of the table and on the sideboard.

RIGHT Olga Polizzi bought a few of the original contents of the house, including the estate maps, which hang from rollers on the wall opposite the front door.

Endsleigh was built at the beginning of the 19th century by the sixth Duke and Duchess of Bedford. Although the family owned a third of Devon, the family seat was Woburn Abbey in Bedfordshire, a huge, regimented, Palladian mansion. Money or land being no object, they set about choosing the perfect spot for the Regency aristocrat's version of a West Country vacation home. The site they chose was the sunny side of a steeply wooded valley through which runs the wide, fish-filled ribbon of the River Tamar.

The famous garden designer Humphrey Repton drew up plans for sculpting the landscape into a garden, while the architect Jeffrey Wyatt designed the house. Wyatt's chosen style was the fashionable, fairytale *cottage orné*, an architectural expression of the romantic English attachment to the rural idyll. In fact, the house is far too large to qualify as a cottage, but its exterior is a picturesque confection of frilled gables,

ABOVE Guests arrive at the back of the house, but the main reception rooms are arranged in a row along the front to take advantage of the views. Double doors open from the drawing room into the paneled library, a room furnished with comfortable armchairs and books. Matting rugs are laid over the original floorboards.

RIGHT The drawing room mixes antique pieces, stylishly reupholstered, with new armchairs and sofas in traditional designs from William Yeoward. The close nailing on the armchairs harks back to Regency designs, but the fabric combination of colored velvet with neutral linen is distinctly modern.

tall chimneys, and leaded casement windows. Verandas supported by rough tree trunks and paved with sheep's knucklebones intensify the rustic feel.

Olga Polizzi, daughter of Lord Forte and chief designer for her brother Rocco Forte's expanding hotel empire, already owned a hotel in the West Country, and liked the idea of opening another. When Endsleigh came up for sale, it was not an obvious candidate. Its Grade I listing was likely severely to limit its conversion, and it didn't have enough bedrooms to be strictly viable.

Having once viewed the house, Olga Polizzi says she was drawn back again, and then again. "It is the most extraordinary place, but I really shouldn't have bought it. It was heart over head." In fact, it is the very qualities that make the house such an unlikely business venture that make it such a fine hotel. Its relative shortage of bedrooms—there are sixteen in the main house—means it feels intimate, and its original layout has barely been changed, so the atmosphere is close to that of a private home.

FAR LEFT A cozy sitting room next to the discreet bar was once the Duchess's study and retains its original wallpaper, a little scuffed in places but otherwise intact. The room overlooks a raised area of enclosed garden surrounded by a shallow channel of water, designed so the Duchess could watch her children play while working at her desk.

LEFT The long corridor that links the main house with the nursery wing has been put to good use as a boot room, where a battalion of Hunter Wellington boots in different sizes lines up for the use of guests. Visiting dogs are also catered for; each dog basket has a cushion upholstered in tasteful linen.

BELOW LEFT Some of the bedrooms have beds by Olga Polizzi that look like enormous wing chairs, with padded heads and ends upholstered in linen, made for comfort as much as looks.

RIGHT Hand-painted Regency wallpapers survive in two of the upstairs bedrooms and look almost modern, thanks to their theatrical scale. Antique furnishings are a mix of the unusual and the practical.

In many ways, a grand Regency house lends itself rather well to the requirements of a modern hotel. Guests can recline on a chaise longue in the library and order tea just as they might have done nearly two centuries ago, or gather in the drawing room for drinks before dinner. All the reception rooms have open fires, and the service cannot have been better when the Duke and Duchess took their seats for dinner.

"We made any changes as gently as we could," says Olga. "We kept and refurbished all the old baths, and we put in old-fashioned cast-iron radiators. Upstairs I used matting because carpet seemed inappropriate. It is a very strong house with its own character, which has to be respected." Three rooms retain their original wallcoverings, painted chinoiserie birds, flowers, and butterflies in bedrooms and an exotic tree-of-life hand-blocked print in the Duchess's study.

Into this beautifully restored, period shell, Olga has introduced her own brand of contemporary glamour. She bought with the house a small selection of the original furnishings. The remainder sold for nearly £650,000. She replaced these with similar antiques, minus the expensive provenance, and mixed them with contemporary armchairs and sofas, pieces of her own design, and quirky things bought "because I thought they were rather beautiful." To adorn the brackets and shelves in the drawing room, she commissioned a series of simple white plates, pitchers, and vases from a favorite potter, Cecile Johnson Soliz.

Luxury hotels are in Olga Polizzi's blood and designing interiors with comfort and practicality uppermost is second nature. The result at Endsleigh is a relaxed, updated version of English country-house style.

COUNTRY LEGACY

"A friend came to stay last summer and said, 'You are living in paradise.' I laughed. There is too much work and worry for paradise." You can see what the friend meant. Catrina Knight-Bruce and her husband Robin inherited a large country house on the side of a secluded Devon valley with views over uninterrupted countryside to the distant blur of Exeter. Gently sloping lawns, mature trees, and a small lake fold around the front of the house. At the back, behind the cobbled stableyard, is a walled garden of espaliered fruit trees, clipped box, vegetables, fruit frames, and flowers intersected by the geometry of gravel paths. There are ponies in the cob-walled paddock, and a flurry of four dogs, one each for Catrina and her three children.

Rounding off this storybook perfection are the playhouses and summerhouses; a tiny wooden cottage under a tree at the edge of the front lawns; an overgrown Queen Anne dollhouse in a corner of the walled garden, with painted brickwork and a paneled front door; a rustic thatched retreat framed by greenery on the edge of the lake; and a neat little clapboard building with French doors, just the right size for a home office, with a view of fields.

These delightful buildings are the family business, established by Robin when he abandoned a career in finance to live in the house bought and extended by his great-great-grandparents. He and Catrina run the business together. On top of managing what is

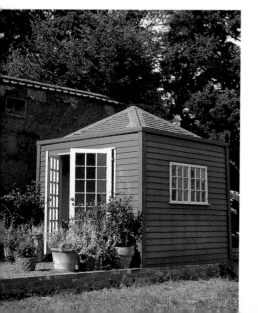

LEFT AND ABOVE The family business has expanded from elaborate playhouses for children to include outdoor dens or home offices for adults, like this clapboard prototype, which sits in a corner of the paddock. At the front of the house there is a tiled terrace outside the original front door, big enough for a table and chairs and with steps leading down to the lawn.

RIGHT When Robin Knight-Bruce's great-great-grandparents bought the house, it was a double-fronted Regency villa. In the late 19th century, it was substantially altered, and a new front entrance was created where the extension housing the billiard room joined the main house. The elaborately carved paneling and chimney pieces also date from this period.

effectively a small estate, with its horses and gardens, and their work as joint Masters of the local hunt, this is what Catrina means by "too much work and worry." "I was thinking the other day," she muses, "how amazed Robin's grandparents would be to see how we still live in the house in much the same way they did. The big difference, however, is that we don't have all the staff they had. We do have help, but it's never enough."

The house looks Victorian, red brick with bay windows and a raised terrace at the front draped in clematis and wisteria. Framed drawings in the staircase hall show the house before it was extended in the late 19th century: a pretty, double-fronted Regency villa. Alterations were restricted to the front façade and the grandiose addition of a wing containing a billiard room, that essential of genteel late Victorian life. Inside, the estate carpenter

ABOVE Next to the kitchen is a pretty, informal dining room, with the Victorian pine table from which they copied the legs for the new work table in the kitchen (see left). Likewise, the glazed china cupboards, also original, inspired the style of the new kitchen cupboards. The Edwardian highchair is used by young guests.

LEFT The kitchen is at the back of the house and leads off a paneled back hall. When Robin and Catrina took on the house, it had been rented for fifteen years to students from Exeter University, and the kitchen was particularly insalubrious. They designed new cupboards and a central work table in the style of a freestanding Victorian kitchen, to look contemporary with the architecture of the house.

RIGHT The formal dining room at the front of the house is reserved for special occasions such as Christmas, when its Victorian paneling and period furnishings make the perfect backdrop.

ABOVE When the house was remodeled in the 19th century, the Regency staircase was replaced by a heavier, more elaborate oak staircase, made by a local carpenter. More recently, the staircase was restored by one of his descendants, who still lives locally. The drawing room leads off this front staircase hall to the left, the dining room to the right. A row of hooks stores leashes for all four dogs.

LEFT In contrast to the heavy, more masculine paneling and dark colors of the dining room, the drawing room, traditionally the room to which ladies withdrew after dinner while gentlemen smoked cigars and talked politics, has a light, pretty feel. Walls are painted duck-egg blue, and an enormous bay window, the late Victorian equivalent of a picture window, looks out across the garden to the countryside beyond. The door opposite the window opens onto the back hall with its late Victorian stained-glass windows.

RIGHT The drawing room largely escaped the architectural additions of the late Victorian makeover and retains a more Regency feel. Furnishings and paintings are mostly inherited pieces, while smaller items have been collected over the years by Catrina, many bought in nearby Taunton Antiques Market.

installed oak paneling in the back hall and dining room and a chunky carved staircase.

When they first visited the house with a view to moving there, it had been rented out as student accommodation for the previous fifteen years. "It was the middle of winter, and a group of students had pulled a huge tree trunk into the room that is now our dining room and were feeding it bit by bit into the fireplace to burn," Catrina laughs. "They were all sitting around huddled in blankets, and the kitchen was stacked with plates and the moldering remains of meals. It was pretty depressing."

Undeterred, Robin and Catrina decided to restore the house as a family home and began a wholesale redecoration. They put in a new kitchen and bathrooms, added a second window to alleviate the gloom of the back hall, and built what Catrina calls a "lean-to" across the rear façade. A realtor might call it a conservatory, but this is distinctly useful, as opposed to decorative, space, an essential buffer zone between indoors and outdoors where Wellington boots and riding boots stand in muddy lines, coats hang, dogs sleep, hats are thrown, pots are stacked,

umbrellas propped. Also at the back of the house are the kitchen and a snug sitting room, and a powder room where an old Silver Cross baby buggy stands, stacked with lampshades.

Both in its layout and its decoration, the house reflects a very traditional English way of life in the country. Even the billiard room still contains a billiard table. The drawing room and dining room at the front of the house have a slightly old-fashioned formal feel, the one more feminine with pale blue walls, gilt-framed paintings, pretty china, and inherited antique furniture, the other with a long table and leather-upholstered chairs watched over by oil paintings of ancestors. Upstairs the bedrooms are pretty with chintz curtains, dressing tables frilled with white voile, flowery china, and Regency watercolors; bathrooms are spacious, carpeted, comfortably furnished rooms, as pioneered in this country by Nancy Lancaster.

ABOVE In the main bedroom, chinoiserie furnishings, including a painted chest of drawers, a rococo wall sconce, and a set of sepia prints, are reflected in the choice of fabric, a chinoiserie chintz used to make the headboard, cushions, and curtains.

LEFT All the bedrooms feature a classic English combination of flowery chintz, antique furniture, and an emphasis on comfort. Ample space means each has a dressing table at the window for the best light, a cushioned armchair, and plenty of storage.

RIGHT Bathrooms follow the same format of traditional comfort and convenience. In the main bathroom, pipes from the washbasin and the toilet are boxed in, making a useful shelf. The toilet is cunningly disguised as a caned armchair. All the bedrooms and bathrooms upstairs have wall-to-wall carpet, which adds to the feel of padded comfort.

The wing above the billiard room is the domain of the three children. The two older girls, Siena and Vita, are talented riders. Across the posters and other teenage paraphernalia that decorate their walls hang garlands of colored rosettes. Their brother Robert's bedroom is almost as thickly festooned with medals for achievements in athletics. Tucked away downstairs is Catrina's study, crammed with books, pictures, family photographs, cards, and tokens made by the children. There is a chair with a pink cushion and a flowery cloth draped over the desk. The effect is as pretty and as busy as she is.

AT HOME IN HISTORY

It seems perfectly appropriate that a Lancashire-born architectural historian, expert on the Wyatt dynasty of architects, and vice-chair of the Georgian Group, should be living in a charmingly vernacular classical country house in the county of his birth. What is more surprising is the fact that Dr. John Martin Robinson, renowned for his exacting taste and erudition, should have purchased the house without feeling the need to view it first.

"At the time I was living in a little cottage on the coast—I also have a small flat in London— and I was feeling restless," he explains. "I was idly looking in local real estate agents when I came across this house advertised for sale and 'in need of renovation.' I knew the village, but what really attracted me was the fact that the house had not been 'tastefully modernized.' I agreed to buy it on the spot."

Far from modernized, the house had long been rented to a series of eccentric tenants, and then left empty. When John Robinson first saw his new home, the kitchen was derelict, the

LEFT AND RIGHT For a house of modest size, the quality of the architectural detailing is exceptional, including an original chimney piece in the dining room and, facing it, a china cupboard flanked by Corinthian pilasters and surmounted by a broken pediment.

ABOVE The carpenter-turned-architect who designed the house subscribed to various architectural pattern books. The front doorcase, for example, can be traced to a design by James Gibbs.

ABOVE The façade is painted in limewash to a color mixed by Alan Lamb, who worked on the restoration of Uppark. The stone mullions are typical of Lancashire architecture.

bathroom unusable. He was thrilled and delighted. Here were features infinitely more rare and desirable than a functioning oven or flushing toilet: a glorious abundance of period detail including paneling, fireplaces, crown molding, doors, architraves, floorboards, and even a built-in china cupboard in the dining room—all original, all intact.

In addition to an aesthetic appreciation of these architectural details, John Robinson was able to trace their likely provenance. Having written a survey of historic houses in the area, he recognized the stylistic quirks of John Hird, a carpenter who worked with the well-known 18th-century architect John Carr of York before turning his own hand to architecture.

Like most provincial architects of the time working in the fashionable classical idiom, Hird used architectural pattern books, copying designs for moldings, carved details, and fireplaces. The front doorcase of this house, for example, which is amusingly grand in its detail in comparison with its modest size, was taken from James Gibbs's *Book of Architecture* (1728), while the chimney pieces and stair balusters are copied from designs in Batty Langley's *The Builder's Jewel* (1741). Both books were out of date when the house was built in 1767, and in its overall design as well as its detail, the house has the feel of an early Georgian building.

John Robinson relishes the architectural effect of formal classicism interpreted, and in some instances thoroughly misinterpreted, by local craftsmen. Four of his front windows are a perfect illustration of this mix, being an attractive hybrid of the stone mullions that characterize Lancashire houses and the Georgian sashes of a more conventionally classical façade. The result is that, despite its Palladian detailing and perfect symmetry, the house has an appealing informality.

ABOVE The kitchen at the back of the house was virtually unusable, but to John Robinson that was far preferable to somewhere that had been "tastefully modernized." He installed an Aga where once there would have been an open fire and subsequently a range, and uses the mantelshelf above to store a mixture of the purely decorative, such as an ostrich egg, and the useful, including a sheaf of wooden spoons.

RIGHT A trio of window shades at a side window in the library leaves wall space free for John Robinson's collection of architectural drawings.

FAR RIGHT Having restored the original house, John Robinson added new single-story wings on either side, with arched Venetian windows and intersecting Gothic glazing echoing the glazing of the china cupboard in the dining room. One of these wings is a library, a perfect writer's retreat with a large desk in the window overlooking the gardens, and sofas on either side of the fireplace for reading at leisure. The internal architecture of the room was inspired by the work of the Wyatts, a dynasty of nine related architects about whom he has written extensively. Even the shade of green paint is based on a scraping from the library by James Wyatt at Heveningham Hall.

Inside, this combination of the mannered and the casual, the grand and the modest, continues. Symmetrical arrangements of pictures and ornaments emphasize the formality of the various splendid chimney pieces, but are "knocked back" by the casual arrangement of sofas and chairs, or the architectural oddity of ceiling beams. Furnishings are traditional and comfortable, mostly antique and dating from throughout the 18th and 19th centuries. Old rugs or rush matting cover the original floorboards, there is a grandfather clock ticking in the hall, and trays of drinks and glasses are ready to welcome guests in the drawing room.

What you would not know unless you were told is that the two gabled wings that flank the house are new. Designed by architect Michael Haigh, one of them is the library, while its twin is that essential of English country living, a boot room, furnished with Wellington boots, the ironing board, a wheelbarrow, and boxes of kindling.

The two acres of garden are what their owner says Jane Austen would have called "a shrubbery," a rambling, typically English garden. Modestly, John Robinson, who is Maltravers Herald of Arms Extraordinary, a Knight of Malta, and librarian to the Duke of Norfolk as well as an author, describes himself as "keen on gardening in an unskilled way."

ABOVE Opposite the drawing-room fireplace, an early paneled chest holds trays of drinks and glasses. The color of the walls is an ideal foil for the soft glint of antique gilded picture frames.

LEFT The drawing-room walls are painted a rich terracotta red, and the room is dominated by a superb carved stone chimney piece inspired by designs published in a pattern book of 1741. The fabric on the sofa and pillows is Strawberry Hill by Melissa Wyndham.

RIGHT Even the bedrooms have large fireplaces with original chimney pieces. The four-poster in the main bedroom is hung with Carnah by Lelievre, lined with Oak Twig by Colefax and Fowler, and the window curtains are in the same fabric. The wallpaper is Mayfair by Hamilton Weston. The combination of traditional patterns, a rug laid over floorboards, and antique furniture gives a cozily old-fashioned feel.

ENGLISH COUNTRY HOUSE design elements

There is something enduringly appealing about the ideal of the English country house, probably because it perfectly combines the English love of the countryside with an equally English nostalgia for a past of carriages and crinolines, tea and croquet. Although the country houses John Fowler and Nancy Lancaster worked on were generally of a scale and grandeur most of us will only experience after having paid for tickets, many aspects of their approach still have relevance. Their style remains a template for the decoration of expensive country-house hotels, partly because of its emphasis on the comfort and convenience of guests. Many of their ideas about the restoration and conservation of period interiors have become accepted good practice and can be usefully applied to all shapes and sizes of house, from cottages to castles. One of Nancy Lancaster's first "rules" for restoring an old house was that you should "realize its period, feel its personality, and try to bring out its good points." Still undeniably excellent advice. As for the furnishing and decoration, she said that "Understatement is extremely important and crossing too many 't's' and dotting too many 'i's' makes a room look overdone and tiresome." Instead, she recommended "a gentle mixture of furniture" to express "life and continuity."

• RESIST OVER-RESTORATION
Much of the romance of an old house resides in its patina of age. An ill-considered coat of paint or varnish, or the sweep of an electric sander, can obliterate in an instant the beauty of a surface worn smooth by generations of feet and hands, faded by sunlight, softened by dust. Clean it by all means, but gently, and if it is practical to leave well enough alone, this may be the best option.

• FLOORING A country house should be practical as well as beautiful, able to withstand the rigors of children, dogs, and a certain amount of mud. Traditional floorings of wood or stone with rugs, preferably of the faded oriental variety, fulfill both criteria. Reserve the padded luxury of wall-to-wall carpet for bedrooms and bathrooms.

• FIREPLACES Nothing is more welcoming or cheering than a blazing log fire, one of the privileges and essentials of country life. Open up original fireplaces, or install new ones if necessary. Don't

despair if old fireplaces smoke. There is nearly always something that can be done to cure it if you consult a flue specialist.

• FABRICS Nancy Lancaster was famous for her cruelty to fabrics, leaving new slipcovers out in the rain to speed up the process of time-worn continuity, and staining any chintz she deemed too brash in a strong solution of tea. Today many of the best fabric houses have done the distressing for you, with prints that appear rubbed and faded fresh from the bolt.

• AGAS Along with a couple of dogs, an Aga range is the *sine qua non* of the country-house kitchen. Use it to dry out boots, iron napkins, loosen screw-top jars, clean wax off candlesticks—and for cooking.

• FURNITURE Even if no one has ever left you as much as a tea cozy, at least some of your furnishings should have the appearance of venerable heirlooms.

ENGLISH COUNTRY HOUSE finishing touches

Because this is essentially a romantic, even nostalgic style, and best suited to old houses replete with period detail, it is also traditional. This is not a style that easily accommodates glass-topped dining tables or designer coffee tables, and a fat Chesterfield with a baggy slipcover will always be more at home than something boxy and modular covered in cream bouclé. But, as the essence of the country-house style is the appearance, if not always the reality, of slow accretion, flashes of modernity can also be appropriate, and are invariably enlivening, whether the work of a favorite contemporary artist or potter, or a brilliantly practical table lamp or desk chair. Evelyn Waugh describes how Brideshead, that fictionalized ideal of the English stately home, "grew silently with the centuries, catching and keeping the best of each generation." The contents of an English country house are often described as the result of an organic process; in which case, there should always be the glimpse of some green shoots.

• FLOWERS Flower arrangements are best on a grand scale for maximum impact. The look is lavish, but need not cost a fortune. The huge plume of foliage in the hall at Endsleigh was picked from the garden and surrounding countryside.

• DINING The English country house is the last remaining habitat of that increasingly rare room, the formal dining room. Country-house dining requires thick, snowy damask, heavy glasses, a serious array of flatware, and proper china plates (although not every day, of course). The finest antique versions are so expensive that using them might put you off your food, but secondhand silver-plated flatware and table linen are affordable and practical. Antique china is delightful to use, and a mix of different patterns is even nicer than a matching service, but remember that you can't put it in the dishwasher.

• CUSHIONS are not just for show, they are for comfort, and for this reason should never be smaller than 14 inches square. They are also an ideal way to use fragments of antique fabric and trimming.

• PICTURES are a problem unless you have a sizeable budget or a fortunate inheritance. Large, old, good-quality, well-framed oil paintings are inevitably expensive, while reproduction prints and frames are unconvincing. Good contemporary art is a better option, and can "lift" an otherwise traditional interior from ordinary to interesting.

• BEDS Modern bed designs often don't look right in country-house bedrooms, and this is usually because they are too low. For a bed to be properly impressive, its mattress should be a minimum of 28 inches above the ground.

• BOOTS However small your English-style country house, you need space for wet coats and muddy boots. A dedicated boot room is ideal; otherwise, you can line a hall or corridor with rows of hooks and shoe racks. A capacious cupboard, complete with good ventilation, is useful for hiding the overflow and ugly sneakers.

• ANIMALS You can just about get away with not having a horse, but not having a dog, whether you like them or not, is unacceptable. Speaking from experience, familiarity breeds adoration, even in an inveterate dog disliker.

Classic
English

The houses on the following pages are not strictly classical, either architecturally or in the way they are furnished, but all owe a debt to classical principles. One house is 1920's neo-Georgian on the outside, with early Georgian features added inside, plus some witty decorative references to the classical style of Vanbrugh. One has an interior inspired by Regency architect Sir John Soane. One is a flat in an early 18th-century house, one a mid-19th-century townhouse. In all cases the rules have been cheerfully adjusted, and the results are as individual as they are charming.

LEFT The window above the sink once looked onto the shady side where the scullery of this London row house reached into the garden. When Nicolette and Maurice first extended into the side, they stopped just short of the window. More recently they added a few more feet, so the window now overlooks an extra patch of reclaimed indoor space.

RIGHT The kitchen table stands in the old side return, and is overlooked by the study window. In a small house, this has transformed a narrow kitchen and scullery into one large, light room. The ceiling height is magnified by vertical matchboarding and the floor area by uninterrupted slate flagstones. The lack of pictures or other extraneous decoration provides a visual contrast to the clustering of objects in other rooms and makes the space feel calm and serene.

SMALL AND BEAUTIFUL

If ever a house should have stretch marks, this is the one. Somewhere toward one end of a gently curved row of houses in fashionable Notting Hill, the frontage is not much wider than a mini-van, the front door is slim for its height, and the hall is barely wider. Originally there were two rooms on each of the three floors and a two-story extension at the back housing kitchen, scullery, and another bedroom above.

Into this small, pretty, urban cottage is slotted a family with three children and a middle-sized dog. It also contains a home office, and enough books and pictures to fill that mini-van to bursting.

Rather than feeling uncomfortably crowded, the house has a pleasing air of serenity. The hall may be narrow, but it displays on one wall a perfectly tessellated gallery of 18th-century black-and-white prints and engravings, a monochrome patchwork of classical motifs stretching from knee-height to ceiling, which announces a certain discipline and order. To the left is the diminutive drawing room

and the study with its lining of shelves, and ahead is the kitchen, bright with sunshine from a glass roof and French doors, and offering an unfeasibly empty expanse of slate flooring.

The house belongs to Nicolette Le Pelley, former Deputy Editor of *The World of Interiors* magazine, and her husband Maurice Fraser, who teaches European politics at the London School of Economics and whose mother is one of the longest-serving antique dealers on Portobello Road. They bought the house fifteen years ago, before the arrival of children, dog, and the need for a home office.

ABOVE The sofa opposite the fireplace is a wooden garden bench, repainted and generously cushioned with striped and checked cotton from Ian Mankin. The prints above were bought mostly in Portobello Market.

LEFT Left of the hall is the drawing room, which was originally separated from the back room, now a library, by double doors. The library tends to overflow, hence the stack of books. On a cupboard fitted in the fireplace alcove is a display of antiquities including a Roman terracotta head, Mesopotamian plates, and a Greek terracotta figure. The painting above is an 18th-century oil of Cleopatra's feast, and over the fireplace is the Sibylla Europa. "As Maurice teaches European politics, he was keen to have her presiding over the room," says Nicolette.

"It was pretty revolting," Nicolette recalls. "A squatter had been camping out on the top floor, and the whole place was filthy and falling to bits." The advantage, as is so often the case with a house that has been long neglected, was that all the original fireplaces and woodwork were intact, ready to be unearthed from behind plywood and rejuvenated.

Once restored, its perfectly formed, modestly proportioned rooms became the ideal backdrop for Nicolette and Maurice's collection of antiques: the prints and engravings they bought together and framed using old frames cut down to fit; the early Delft pottery that Nicolette loves; the antiquities that Maurice has bought and sold since childhood; and the oil paintings of Sibyls, those revered soothsaying women of classical legend. "Maurice is crazy about them. He likes intellectual women," laughs Nicolette, too modest to add that she is one herself.

Sadly, she says, their buying days are now over. "We have pushed this house to its limits," she adds. "The only answer is not to buy anything." The pushing began when they glassed over part of the side return. Initially this was space required for Nicolette's home office. With friend and business partner Cheryl Knorr, Nicolette runs a website, House &

LEFT The stairs, bedroom, landing, and bathroom are all carpeted with seagrass matting. The walls in the bathroom are Dulux latex in Brilliant White, and therefore "nice and easy to repaint fairly frequently."

RIGHT Another of Maurice's beloved Sybils watches over the main bedroom, in this instance the Sibylla Persica, painted in the 19th century after Domenichino. Paint colors are two shades of white by Farrow and Ball, Off White on the walls and Hardwick White on the woodwork. The gilded stars and the gold foil wreath on the mantelpiece are both props from the days when Nicolette worked for *The World of Interiors* magazine.

Garden Addresses, a directory of suppliers for interiors and gardens, and the answer to all manner of decorating quests, from where to find antique ticking to the best modern faucets.

When another bedroom was required for child number three, they moved the drawing room downstairs and lost a dining room. Nicolette's office made way for a kitchen table, and she moved her files into a tiny room built above the very end of the kitchen extension and reached by wooden steps outside the kitchen door. More recently, they shunted the side-return extension out another few feet to reach the end wall. "We needed it for the dog," claims Nicolette. This is as far as the house can expand, leaving a lush nook of a backyard.

Despite the incremental way the house has grown, its contents and decoration have maintained a calm uniformity. Seagrass matting flows from hall into the drawing room, up the stairs, and into the bedrooms, and plain paint throughout is limited to white, off-white, and dusky green. And although some walls are crammed with pictures, others are left completely bare. There is minimal pattern: fabrics are almost exclusively stripes and checks, and ornaments are carefully corraled in beautifully arranged still lifes on mantelpieces and shelves.

Tucked discreetly behind the front door, on a row of coat hooks, hang three mini-scooters. "Well, where else could I put them?" asks Nicolette. It's a fair point.

RIGHT The house is bursting with pictures and books, and every mantelpiece, including that in the library, doubles as extra book shelving. Old leather bindings mean that these volumes are also decorative.

LEFT The living room still has its original plain fielded paneling and refined gray marble fireplace, although the mantelpiece is later, as is the infill to make a smaller grate. The room has been divided to make a separate kitchen, but Ben Pentreath has elegantly shoehorned a surprising amount into a limited space, including two small but comfortable Victorian armchairs, which he has upholstered in men's suiting from the tailor around the corner. Empty frames on either side of the mirror surround postcards pinned to the wall, making an arrangement of pleasing symmetry.

RIGHT "Good art" is Ben Pentreath's idea of real luxury. His own collection includes woodcuts, drawings, photographs, and this dramatic oil painting of a stormy landscape by Tai-Shan Schierenberg. The mugs on the mantelpiece are early 19th-century Mocha pottery; their fernlike patterns were made by dropping an unsavory infusion of tobacco juice in stale urine onto the wet glaze before firing.

SINGULAR STYLE

High on the wall in the tiny inner hall of Ben Pentreath's Bloomsbury flat is a drawing of a double-fronted house designed for a "Captain Pentreath." It looks Regency, a record of an elegant family home. "I drew that for my parents when I was seventeen," Ben Pentreath confesses. "But it was never built." The drawing is evidence of an early fascination with architecture, particularly of the classical sort. "My father was based at the Royal Naval College in Greenwich, where we lived, so I was brought up surrounded by the most sublime Christopher Wren buildings."

RIGHT Open shelves along one wall of the narrow kitchen store china, an attractive mix of the old and new. The walls above are filled with posters reflecting Ben's love of typography.

FAR RIGHT A small round table, draped in a sober gray flannel cloth, sits between the windows and allows more seating space than an equivalent square or rectangular table. The pair of dining chairs is English 18th century.

OPPOSITE The wall that divides the kitchen from the living room is covered by a tessellation of framed maps of London, first published in 1745 and showing the house when there were still fields on the other side of the road. The large sofa has had a makeover, with new wooden legs replacing its more contemporary metal legs, and is upholstered in herringbone wool from Ian Mankin. With no wall space for curtains, Ben Pentreath chose simple ruched blinds in a masculine stripe.

BELOW The map above the sofa works both as a fascinating conversation piece—it is impossible not to pore over it looking for particular streets and familiar places—and as a decorative device. Its delicacy and lightness, and the reflective quality of the glass, help to minimize the intrusion of the wall.

He majored in History of Art at Edinburgh University and began his architectural training working with Charles Morris in Norfolk. This was followed by five years in New York, working on "lavish, American classical houses—glossy, luxurious versions of the English country house."

Back in London in 2004, he set up his own company, Working Group. "Most of our work is on fairly large housing projects. We design in traditional styles, not simply as an aesthetic choice, but because we believe they are sustainable and practical. We don't over-use glass, for example, but stick to the tried and trusted ratio of between fifteen and twenty percent window to wall."

This last comment is made as he gestures toward his own living-room windows, a pair of sashes that date back to 1720. For an architectural classicist, this flat has obvious appeal, being on the second floor of a house in an early Georgian row of houses. Ben Pentreath's tastes and enthusiasms are announced even before you step inside. Out on the sidewalk a small garden of pots burgeons around the doorstep, and a number of his prints and engravings have crept out onto the walls of the communal staircase.

Once through his front door, you enter the tiny inner hall, with a living room to your left and a bedroom to your right. Beyond the bedroom is a very small bathroom, and next to the living room

is a narrow kitchen. The space is limited, cramped even, but Ben Pentreath has furnished it so carefully that it feels the perfect size for its contents.

The living room retains its 18th-century plain, fielded paneling and refined gray marble fireplace, which had been painted and which Ben painstakingly stripped. The room is divided by a wall, which separates one of the three windows, to make a kitchen. Covering this wall is a reproduction of a map, first published in 1745, each section framed and closely hung like a large, simple jigsaw. The map shows the street where Ben lives as it was when newly built on the edge of fields. And, being black and white and delicate in its detail, the map serves to lighten rather than emphasize the effect of the dividing wall.

Beneath the map is a large, deep sofa, upholstered in masculine gray herringbone tweed, its bulky presence proof that being brave enough to put an oversized piece of furniture in an undersized room has the surprising result of creating a sense of comfortable space. The same is true in the bedroom, which is filled almost to capacity by the four-poster bed that Ben inherited from his grandparents.

In the bedroom there is only space for a chair and chest of drawers, but in the living room the sofa is nicely balanced by two neat armchairs, which face it, and the visual weight of a bookcase reaching up to the ceiling in the alcove next to the fireplace. He has even squeezed in a table and two chairs between the windows.

Despite the fact that the original proportions of this room have been compromised by the necessity of the new kitchen wall, Ben has managed to preserve its dignity. There are enough pairings and symmetries to give it some formal elegance, and there are enough mismatchings—the cushions, the armchairs—for visual variety and the comfort that goes with a lack of formality.

"Comfort is very important," Ben agrees, "but to me it is about much more than sofas. To me real luxury is about having good art on the walls." And here he has that, too—a stormy landscape by Tai-Shan Schierenberg, woodcuts by Eric Ravilious, and a photograph of a Devon landscape by his son James Ravilious among other, mostly 20th-century works. It's amazing how many good things you can fit into a small space.

ABOVE Using open shelving for storage, both in the kitchen and the tiny bathroom, is one of the ways Ben Pentreath has managed to create an illusion of space. It also helps to have the eye and the discipline to keep their contents as good-looking as this.

LEFT While the small living room contains a noticeably large sofa, the even smaller bedroom is practically filled by a four-poster bed, which Ben Pentreath inherited from his grandparents. He hung the simple wooden frame himself, with double-sided wool from Colefax and Fowler that is so thick and closely woven he has not bothered to hem its edges. The original paneling is painted a soft gray, against which the warm tomato red of the wool looks rich and cozy. In fact, he says it is a very drafty room, thanks to its poorly fitting sash window, so the curtains have a practical as well as a decorative function.

Even in the tiny bathroom Ben Pentreath has found space for a display of symmetry, with white china candlesticks on each side of a pot of white geraniums on a painted chest. Flooded with light and decorated in shades of white, the effect is bright and clean.

CLASSICAL ILLUSION

Whenever the English adopt a style, whether rococo or Palladianism, the result tends to be a more understated version of the original. Garden and exhibition designer George Carter is perfectly capable of grand gestures when required—whether ten-foot obelisks for an exhibition at the Queen's Gallery or a pastiche baroque frontage in painted plywood to disguise a tool shed.

BELOW The red-brick pantiled house was built in neat, modest, country Georgian style in 1920 for a tenant farmer. George Carter designed a garden to complement and frame its architecture. The pair of elongated urns in the foreground once graced the parapet of a bank.

A view from the end of the front hall into the drawing room, where a gateleg table, slightly sagging chair, and old-fashioned telephone constitute one of several places to work in the house, a convenience George finds necessary despite having a "proper" office in its own room at the back.

Recent exhibitions he has worked on include *Fabergé* and *George III*, also at Buckingham Palace, and he is a Chelsea Flower Show Gold Medal winner. In his house in the middle of Norfolk farmland, George Carter's taste for classical design and his penchant for the exuberant flourish of baroque have been toned and scaled down to a quaint elegance that is as comfortable to live with as it is pleasurable to look at.

The house itself typifies the modest "neo-Georgian" type of classicism that remains popular for new houses in English towns and villages to this day. But for the plaque on the side announcing that it was built in 1920, you would think it a good two centuries old. The quiet formality of the architecture is emphasized by the garden that George Carter has designed to surround it, with its straight-edged walls of hedge, pairs of urns, and crisp vistas. Expanses of

On the other side of the striped sofa from the table and telephone is the sitting end of the drawing room. The sofa, designed by George Carter with a low back, marks the line where a wall once divided the room in two. The paneling surrounding the fireplace was added by George Carter, incorporating cupboard doors from another house.

LEFT Regency and Georgian decanters, with and without their stoppers, add sparkle to a tabletop in the corner of the dining room. The table itself, with its antiqued mirror back, was designed by George Carter and incorporates a charming visual conceit, as the half-urn is reflected in the mirror to look whole.

lawn and gravel and the notable absence of flowerbeds give the garden a minimalist serenity that you might expect to be continued in the house.

In fact, the interior is far from minimal. If china, glass, pictures, books, and ornaments are the interior design equivalent of flowers, these rooms are herbaceous borders bursting with variety, albeit carefully color-coordinated. Built on a large estate for a tenant farmer, the house has the proportions of a cottage, with small rooms, relatively low ceilings, and a steep staircase. Into three rooms downstairs and four plus bathroom upstairs, George Carter has crammed the fruits of a lifetime of collecting; every surface and shelf has its considered tableau of monochrome New Hall china, Regency decanters, 18th-century creamware, luster teacups, blue-and-white china, Georgian cut glass, Sheffield plate, fragments of sculpture, and casts of architectural details. Books have escaped from the upstairs library shelves to form pillars and columns by beds and chairs, and pictures group in clusters on the walls.

Although the house is full and rather small, there is nevertheless a pleasing sense of order and coherence, and a surprising effect of spaciousness. This is partly due to the restrained color palette of blues and grays, whites and creams, which extends from paintwork to furnishings and to objects themselves. Even the pictures on the walls are predominantly black-and-white engravings, and what color there is— whether in the rugs that cover the matting or the upholstery of a chair— is faded and bleached with time and use, and "slightly scruffy around the edges," which, as George Carter says, is "how we English like it."

Soft, pale colors provide a visual coherence, while a judicious use of symmetry provides the sense of order and calm. Every room has its focus of perfectly balanced objects, whether a group of pictures, or china laid out on a tabletop. Each mantelpiece is a satisfying arrangement of pairs of items, on one obelisks, on another saucers, placed either side

The dining room is painted in an indefinable shade of dull green, the subtle result of "mixing thousands of tins of paint I had left over," says George Carter. The carved lettering over the fireplace is student work from the 1940s, one of several things he rescued from a dumpster when he was a student of fine art at Newcastle and the university was busy "modernizing" and clearing out its cast room.

ADJUTORIUM NOSTRUM
IN NOMINE DOMINI

LEFT Most of the furniture in the house is from the 18th or early 19th century, like the graceful Regency chaise longue, upholstered in ticking, which sits in the window of the drawing room and seems to invite long afternoons of languorous reading. The effect, however, is far from fusty or old-fashioned, partly because, although the house is full of things, there are always plenty of breathing spaces in between, with plain walls, a minimum of pattern, and a disciplined palette of muted colors.

RIGHT The cherrywood bateau lit in the main bedroom dates from 1840, which could almost be defined as the cut-off date for George Carter's taste in 19th-century antiques. A simple stool serves as a bedside table, and there are usually several columns of books lined up within easy reach of the bed. The flooring is matting with rugs laid over it.

of a central piece. The drawing room was apparently a challenge in terms of balance. "It used to be two rooms," George explains, "and the fireplace was not in the middle, which is why I decided to panel the chimney breast and put cupboards on either side so the fact that it is off center is less noticeable."

George also designed the sofa in the drawing room, which acts as a discreet division between the sitting end of the room and the end with a table, chair, and telephone, sometimes used as a home office. "I kept the back of the sofa deliberately low in order not to break up the space," he points out. This attention to scale is key to the spacious feel throughout the house. Most of the furniture is low, and pictures and mirrors are also hung well below ceiling height, giving the impression of extra height.

Color, scale, and proportion come naturally to a designer who spends much of his time thinking about them. But the house also has a style and wit that seem as peculiarly English as the

understatement that comes with things being "slightly scruffy." While most of his furnishings and possessions have the refinement typical of Georgian and Regency design, almost all were bought cheaply, some have been rescued from dumpsters, and others are what George modestly refers to as "cobble-ups."

One particularly inventive "cobble-up" stands on the bedroom mantelpiece, a candelabra (pictured on page 182) assembled by nailing four matching brass door plates to a rectangular wooden block, topped with a ball from a builder's yard, gessoed and gilded, and hung with cut-glass drops and branches that he bought in pieces for less than a pound. He also made the mirror behind it, from scraps of old molding, painted white. Among the more serious "antiques" are little metal gates from old toy farms and painted lead farm animals grazing between the gilt, cut glass, and porcelain. The inspiration behind this house may be classical, but this is classicism at its most domesticated.

ABOVE LEFT The collection of things on the library desk includes George Carter's great-aunt's paintbox.

LEFT An upstairs bedroom doubles as a library, where a leopard-skin rug is spread over a leather consulting couch that George Carter describes as "deeply uncomfortable." The feel of the room is 17th—rather than 18th—century, its tone set by the bolection chimney piece installed by George Carter, its wood painted to look like glossy marble. The room is extremely full, but order is asserted by the arrangement of pictures and china over the fireplace, centered by a Chinese-export plate with an engraving above of King Edward IV's tomb in Westminster Abbey.

ABOVE RIGHT The period mood changes again in a spare bedroom to a subdued 1930's Art Deco, with a bedside table by the Rowley Gallery and a chrome and painted metal bedside lamp. The framed woodcut was done by a child at the Geffrye Museum where, early in his career, George Carter worked helping to arrange exhibitions.

RIGHT The outside privy has been transformed from a plain brick lean-to into a garden pavilion worthy of the 18th-century euphemism "temple of convenience," thanks to the addition of a wooden façade in the style of the early 18th-century architect and playwright, Sir John Vanbrugh. Its exterior forms the "view-stopper" to a long garden vista, but even its interior has been transformed, with a boxed-in cistern, a French metal washstand, and various brackets for oil lights and candles. A temple, indeed.

A Well-balanced Arrangement

Roger Jones is particularly articulate on the subject of English style. Since the mid-1990s he has been head of the antiques department of Colefax and Fowler, presiding over the Brook Street premises of this most English of decorating firms, where charming period rooms display furnishings epitomizing John Fowler's preference for "humble elegance."

"In the context of decorating, 'Perfect English' is something of a contradiction," he comments acutely. "We like our chic to be shabby, our grandeur to be faded—perfection is a very non-English quality."

Verbal precision is as natural to Roger Jones as his eye for a desirable antique. He was recruited into the world of decorating from the unlikely background of the law, exchanging work as a parliamentary counsel for a license to buy "more or less whatever I wanted." His personal taste for understatement and his dislike of ostentation are apparent in the antiques

ABOVE The deep doorway between the living room and the kitchen with its adjacent dining area has been put to good use as shelving for books. The gentle curve of the overdoor is one of the architectural elements introduced by Roger and his architect, inspired by the John Soane fireplace.

LEFT The seminal fireplace, seen on the left, was designed by Georgian architect Sir John Soane for the morning room of Pell Wall Hall in Shropshire and bought by Roger Jones as "a great extravagance." The contents of the room show how a mix of the antique and the contemporary, and the introduction of pieces from other cultures, helps to create a relaxed and informal feel. What unifies these disparate elements—the Regency chair, the modern corner sofa, the painted Indian table, and the abstract art—is color and the careful balancing of scale and proportion.

FAR LEFT On the left of the fireplace is a painted Swedish bookcase. The desk is French Empire, mahogany with ormolu mounts, its wood sun-bleached to the color of honey. Set at right angles between the windows, it is in the best position for natural light.

LEFT Even the bedroom windows at the front have views of greenery, being at just the right height to overlook the canopies of plane trees planted along the road. The striped carpet introduces subtle gradations of color.

RIGHT The main bedroom leads off the hall through a pair of tall double doors, which are mirrored by doors opposite leading into the drawing room. Despite the dominance of the large, high bed, the room has a slightly masculine dignity that makes it seem equally appropriate for daytime use. This is partly due to the formal symmetry of the arrangements and also to the lack of obvious bedroom furnishings. The clothes "closets" on either side of the antique chimney piece, for example, are French bookshelves, their contents hidden by gathered fabric behind the glass.

he buys to sell and, perhaps more tellingly, in the way he has designed and decorated his own Kensington flat.

He bought the flat in 1998, seduced by the view of trees and sky from the back windows, where long gardens merge into park. It occupies the second floor of an 1850's house in a grand street and had been clumsily converted. With the help of architect Giles Vincent, Roger gutted and rearranged the space, restoring its architectural integrity and adding some of his own invention.

The first and most extravagant item he bought for the flat was a chimney piece by Sir John Soane. More than a focus for the living room, this arrestingly beautiful piece of white marble became the architectural muse for the whole flat, inspiring the choice of crown moldings, the high baseboards, the domed ceiling of the entrance hall, and the gentle arches over the doors and the bed alcove. Roger also added two pairs of tall double doors and new floorboards.

All this change, all these additions, and yet the rooms have a patina and air of permanence more usually lost on a dumpster. Roger Jones' efforts to make sure that his home has a "studied casualness, and the appearance of having evolved rather than been designed" have paid off. Where possible, architectural features are reclaimed, ready-weathered by time and use. Paint colors are faded and indefinable, and the new doors are poplar, expertly grained to look like sun-bleached mahogany.

LEFT The sofa in the main bedroom plays a double role as bed-end and seating and gives the room another purpose as a cozy sitting room. Building closets on either side of the bed created an alcove for the bed to sit in and added shelving and storage. Matching the closet doors to the door into the bathroom gives the room architectural unity and creates an impression of rooms beyond.

ABOVE RIGHT The bathroom has a grandeur not commensurate with its size, thanks to architectural detailing such as the shallow-arched alcove enclosing the bathtub and the limestone surround and wall tiling, cut to accommodate the faucets.

RIGHT As in the bathroom, mirror covers a wall in the small entrance hall. As you step into the flat, space seems to open up around you.

As for the contents of the rooms, his work gives him the opportunity for endless refinement. The living room contains some fine English antiques, but also pieces from other countries. The painted bookcase on the left of the fireplace is Swedish, and over the English oak bookcase hang pictures of Indian elephants, musicians, and dancers. And, while most of the furniture is old, a trio of striking abstract paintings hangs over the corner sofa. "Mixing modern or more ethnic things helps to 'knock back' a room furnished with antiques, makes it feel more relaxed and less rigid," says Roger.

A similar balance must be found, he thinks, between symmetry and asymmetry. Too much symmetry, and a room can look stiff and contrived; too little or none at all, and the effect is unnervingly random. With endearing modesty Roger Jones claims that he is still not entirely happy with the furnishing of his sitting room in this respect. "I think it might be cured by increasing the symmetry quotient, perhaps with a pair of armchairs."

He is more pleased with the bedroom, with its three powerful symmetries centering on the fireplace, the bed, and the pair of sash windows. Visual order thus established, the differences in scale between the high double doors and the small door into the bathroom, or the chairs on either side of the painted chest, are interesting rather than jarring.

The last area of decoration that requires careful balance, according to Roger, is that between having too few possessions, which can look bland, and too much clutter. He also insists that, whatever the style of an interior, it should provide an appropriate setting for its occupants' way of life. "Extremes such as baroque and minimalism are too self-conscious," he says. Not only is Roger Jones articulate both verbally and visually, he is also refreshingly practical.

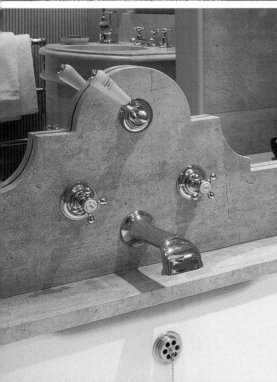

CLASSIC ENGLISH design elements

The classical ideal of the Italian Renaissance, it was claimed, was based on laws of architectural harmony, handed down from the Greeks and Romans and made newly accessible by Andrea Palladio's writings in the 16th century. While the Renaissance was busy flourishing in Italy and spreading its pillars, porticoes, and proportions across the rest of Europe, England remained stubbornly immune to the splendors of classical architecture. It wasn't until the 18th century that the classical ideal finally took hold in England, despite attempts to introduce it nearly a hundred years before by early exponents such as the architect Inigo Jones. Even after "The Rule of Taste," as it was known, became the prevailing fashion for architecture, it was applied in a recognizably English idiom. The poet Alexander Pope, that great arbiter of English taste and morals, recommended in one of his *Moral Essays* using "good sense" and sensitivity to natural surroundings when building in the classical style, ridiculing the self-importance of triumphal arches as models for "a garden gate" and the pretension of dining rooms designed in imitation of "temples" and "hecatombs." From the heights of intellectual commentary to the labors of the jobbing builder, the English response to classicism was to avoid pomposity and to adjust its rules to make it appropriate for use, whether for the design of a comfortable drawing room or a fashionable ballroom. This domesticated, colloquial classicism is the familiar and perennially popular style we now know as Georgian.

• SYMMETRY Vernacular and modernist buildings favor asymmetry, but classicism puts symmetry at the top of its aesthetic priorities. There is no doubt that symmetry is pleasing to the eye, whether found in a human face or the arrangement of ornaments on a mantelshelf. A room with no symmetry can seem nervy and visually irritating, but you can also have too much of a good thing.

• BALANCE Getting the right balance between symmetry and asymmetry in a room may be the key to its visual success. Unfortunately, there is no magic formula, and like so many aspects of interior decoration, getting it just right is often a question of trial and error, instinct and "eye."

• PROPORTIONS were central to the ideals of classical architecture. Andrea Palladio's seven ideal room proportions, published in his *Four Books*

of Architecture in 1570, were endlessly adopted and adapted by architects and builders working in the classical style. Few of us will ever occupy rooms conforming to these ideal proportions, but there are various visual tricks that can improve bad proportions in a room. For example, different window treatments can adjust the apparent shape of an opening. A window's height can be raised by hanging a Roman shade on the wall above it, while its width can be narrowed by hanging curtains on a shorter rod. A ceiling that is too high can be lowered by adding a picture or dado rail or both, while wallpaper with vertical stripes can make a low ceiling appear higher.

• FURNISHINGS should have a more vertical than horizontal emphasis. Low-slung sofas, chairs, coffee tables, and beds look too casual and modern.

CLASSIC ENGLISH finishing touches

Throughout the 18th century, a classical education was the mark of a man of taste and good breeding. Both Latin and Greek were taught as second languages, and an extended visit to the European continent to see its principal cities and sights, known as the Grand Tour, was considered an essential experience for a young gentleman. Ruins, especially of the classical variety, were top of the travel agenda and were considered both picturesque and salutary, reminders of how even the greatest endeavors of men eventually crumble to dust. Those who could afford it brought back with them genuine antiquities such as Roman statuary to adorn their neo-Palladian mansions, while a huge industry grew up selling reproduction classical artifacts as souvenirs for the less-well-heeled visitor, from busts to cameos. Something of this intellectual and aesthetic one-upmanship still clings to the classically inspired interior. This is English style at its more formal and cerebral, dressed for dinner and ready to engage in sophisticated conversation. It also happens (as a non sequitur!) to be English style at its most masculine.

• PAIRS Buying things in pairs, whether candlesticks, table lamps, cushions, pictures, or chairs, is an excellent way to make sure your rooms will have the requisite dose of symmetry.

• PICTURES The 18th century was the great age of the print, when an artist like William Hogarth could achieve huge popularity with a series of engravings such as *The Rake's Progress*, providing affordable art for mass consumption. Antique prints are still a relatively inexpensive way to adorn a wall and have a restrained, formal feel, especially when grouped symmetrically. Old frames always look better than new, but add to the cost. If you are having an old print newly framed, a slim, plain black frame looks best.

• ANTIQUITIES Genuine antiquities, such as those in Nicolette Le Pelley's house, vary hugely in price from the prohibitively extravagant to the surprisingly affordable. Alternatively, museums such as the British Museum sell good casts of originals, from busts to bas-reliefs.

• FABRICS This is one English style for which floral fabrics are not appropriate. Stripes and sophisticated checks have a suitably chic and restrained elegance. Ben Pentreath used men's suiting as upholstery to good effect. If you crave pattern, there are some wonderful classically inspired toiles de Jouy, which look particularly good mixed with checks and stripes, as on Nicolette Le Pelley's sofa.

• ORNAMENTS It is not difficult to find ornaments with a classical feel. George Carter collects New Hall porcelain, produced in large quantities at the turn of the 18th century and particularly elegant in black, white, and gold, but there are many other more recent and quite common designs, such as plain white china with black or gold Greek key pattern borders, or transfer-printed classical scenes. Wedgwood, the pottery that made its name reproducing classical vases, is now reintroducing many of its original 18th-century designs.

• CANDLELIGHT The Age of Elegance was lit by candles, still the most flattering light of all. Candlesticks modeled on classical columns in china or metal, new or old, are not hard to find. Grouped together they can look like miniature ruins and, once lit, will provide a warm, bright glow.

DIRECTORY

ARCHITECTURAL SALVAGE

ARCHITECTURAL ACCENTS
2711 Piedmont Road NE
Atlanta, GA 30305
404-266-8700
www.architectural accents.com
*Antique light fixtures, door
hardware, garden antiques,
and other reclaimed items.*

ARCHITECTURAL ANTIQUES
1900 Linwood Avenue
Oklahoma City, OK 73109
405-232-0759
*A wide range of architectural
salvage.*

THE ARCHITECTURAL BANK
1824 Felicity
New Orleans, LA 2702
504-523-2702
Historic salvage for your home.

OLD THEATRE
ARCHITECTURAL SALVAGE
2045 Broadway
Kansas City, MO 64108
816-283-3740
rick@architecturalsalvage.com
*Think of your home as a theater and
bring home some architectural drama.*

SALVAGE ONE/CHICAGO
Architectural Salvage Company
1524 South Sangamon
Chicago, IL 60608
312-733-0098
Architectural artifacts.

UNITED HOUSE WRECKING
CORPORATION
535 Hope Street
Stamford, CT 06906
203-348-5371
*Architectural fragments from
old houses.*

FURNITURE AND
FINISHING TOUCHES:
ANTIQUE AND
TRADITIONAL

THE BOMBAY COMPANY, INC.
P.O. Box 161009
Fort Worth, TX 76161
Call 800-829-7789 or visit
www.bombaycompany.com
to find a store near you.
*Reproductions of classic, often
British colonial-style home
furnishings and accessories.*

CLINTON HOWELL
ANTIQUES
19 East 74th Street
New York, NY 10021
212-517-5879
*English and continental furniture
and decorative arts from the 17th
to the 20th centuries.*

COUNTRY GARDEN
ANTIQUES
147 Parkhouse
Dallas, TX 75207
214-741-9331
*Shabby chic antiques to help you
achieve an English cottage style.*

THE CRAFTSMAN HOME
3048 Claremont Avenue
Berkeley, CA 94705
510-633-6503
www.craftsmanhome.com
*Arts and Crafts period and revival
home furnishings.*

DUCCI
L.no Corsini 24/r
50123 Florence, Italy
+39 0552 14550
www.DUCCIshop.com
*The source of Leslie Geddes-
Brown's parchment lampshades,
also wonderful imitation fruits
made from marble.*

THE ECLECTIC COLLECTOR
1201 Lexington Avenue (between
81st and 82nd Streets)
New York, NY 10028
212-249-4277
*18th- and 19th-century continental
antique furniture and decorative arts.*

FLORIAN PAPP
962 Madison Avenue
New York, NY 10021
212-288-6770
*18th- and 19th-century English
and continental furniture from
designers Thomas Chippendale
and William Morris.*

FREDERICK P. VICTORIA
AND SON, INC.
154 East 55th Street
New York, NY 10022
212-755-2549
*English and continental furniture,
clocks, and decorative arts dating
from 1700 to 1830.*

GERALD MURPHY ANTIQUES
60 Main Street South
South Woodbury, CT 06798
203-266-4211
*17th- to 19th-century English
and American furniture, clocks,
barometers, pottery, and glass.*

GEORGE SMITH
73 Spring Street
New York, NY 10012
212-226-4747
www.georgesmith.com
*Capacious and relaxed traditional
sofas and armchairs.*

THE MANHATTAN ARTS
AND ANTIQUES CENTER
1050 Second Avenue at 55th Street
New York, NY 10022
212-355-4400
*Large antiques emporium selling
period furniture, silver clocks,
chandeliers, porcelain, and more.*

NEWEL ART GALLERIES, INC.
423 East 53rd Street
New York, NY 10022
212-758-1970
*A six-story building housing
antiques from many periods
and nations.*

RICHARD B. ARKWAY
59 East 54th Street
New York, NY 10022
212-751-8135
*Antique maps, globes, atlases,
rare books, and other curiosities.*

SALISBURY ANTIQUES
CENTER
46 Library Street (off Route 44)
Salisbury, CT 06068
860-433-0424
*Formal and country-style English
and American furniture, silver,
and paintings.*

S. WYLER, INC.
941 Lexington Avenue
New York, NY 10021
212-879-9848
*Antique English silver, Sheffield
plate, Georgian glassware, antique
porcelain (English and Chinese
export).*

FURNITURE AND
FINISHING TOUCHES:
CONTEMPORARY

ABC CARPET & HOME
888 Broadway
New York, NY 10003
212-473-3000
Visit www.ABC.com for a retail
outlet near you.
*An eclectic collection of accessories
for the home, representing all periods
and styles.*

ANTHROPOLOGIE
1700 Sansom Street, 6th floor
Philadelphia, PA 19103
Call 800-309-2500 to find a store
near you or visit
www.anthropologie.com.
*Often vintage-inspired one-of-
a-kind home accessories and
decorative details.*

CHARLES P. ROGERS
55 West 17th Street
New York, NY 10011
212-675-4400
www.charlesprogers.com
*Brass, iron, and wood bed frames,
from classic to contemporary.*

CONRAN SHOP
415 East 59th Street
New York, NY 10022
212-755-7249
www.conran.com
*Tasteful contemporary furniture
and accessories.*

CRATE & BARREL
646 N. Michigan Avenue
Chicago, IL 60611
800-996-9960
Visit www.crateandbarrel.com
for a retail outlet near you.
*Contemporary furniture and
accessories for every room.*

DESIGN WITHIN REACH
225 Bush Street, 20th Floor
San Francisco, CA 94104
Call 800-944-2233 or visit
www@dwr.com to find
a retail outlet near you.
*Design Within Reach provides
access to well-designed furnishings
traditionally found only in designers'
showrooms.*

ETHAN ALLEN
Ethan Allen Drive
P.O. Box 1966
Danbury, CT 06813
Call 800-228-9229 or visit
www.ethanallen.com for
a retail outlet near you.
*Classic reproduction furniture
for every room of the home.*

MAINE COTTAGE
FURNITURE
P.O. Box 935
Yarmouth, ME 04096
207-846-7050
Visit www.mainecottage.com
to find a dealer near you.
*Simple, hardworking country-style
furniture for every room.*

WORKBENCH
470 Park Avenue South
New York, NY 10016
Call 800-380-2370 or visit
www.workbenchfurniture.com
for a retail outlet near you.
*Clean and functional modern
furniture for bedrooms, dining, and
living rooms, storage, and more.*

LIGHTING

ANTIQUE LIGHTING
COMPANY
8214 Greenwood Avenue North
Seattle, WA 98103
800-224-7880
www.antiquelighting.com
*Replicas of beautiful antique
fixtures and custom lighting.*

BRASS LIGHT GALLERY
131 South First Street
Milwaukee, WI 53204
800-243-9595
www.brasslight.com
*Residential lighting and vintage
restoration services.*

CONTINUUM ANTIQUES
AND COLLECTIBLES
#7 Route 28
Orleans, MA 02653
508-253-5813
www.oldlamp.com
An antique lighting shop.

GRIFFIN BROTHERS AND
COMPANY
613 New Britain Avenue
Farmington, CT 06032
860-678-9007
www.griffinbros.com
Specializes in lighting restoration.

HISTORIC LIGHTING
114 East Lemon Avenue
Monravia, CA 91016
888-757-9770
www.historiclighting.com
Arts and Crafts revival lighting.

REVIVAL LIGHTING
4860 Rainier Avenue South
Seattle, WA 98118
206-722-4404
www.revivallighting.com
*Large selection of restored vintage
and antique lighting.*

VICTORIAN REVIVAL
416-789-1704
www.victorian-revival.com
*Online purveyor of architectural
antiques, including wall sconces,
hanging fixtures, floor lamps, and
porch lights.*

CARPETS, FABRICS, AND WALLCOVERINGS

BEAUVAIS CARPETS
201 East 57th Street
New York, NY 10022
212-688-2265
*Rare antique and decorative
European and oriental carpets.*

BURROWS STUDIO
SHOWROOM
12 Masonic Place
Provincetown, MA 02657
www.burrows.com
*English Arts and Crafts wallpaper,
including designs by John Dando
Sedding, Aldam Heaton, and CFA
Voysey Art at Home Gallery.*

CHARLES RUPERT
2005 Oak Bay Avenue
Victoria
British Columbia V8R 1ES
Canada
(001) 250-592-4916
www.charlesrupert.com
*William Morris wallpaper and
fabrics, as well as other English
Arts and Crafts designs.*

JAX ARTS & CRAFTS RUGS
109 Parkway
Berea, KY 40403
859-986-5410
www.jaxrugs.com
Arts and Crafts movement rugs.

JR BURROWS AND COMPANY
393 Union Street
P.O. Box 522
Rockland, MA 02370
800-347-1795
www.burrows.com
*William Morris and Wilton and
Brussels carpets, plus the Burrows
studio line of English Arts and
Crafts wallpaper.*

LAURA ASHLEY, INC.
6 St. James Avenue
Boston, MA 02116
Call 800-367-2000 or visit
www.laura-ashleyusa.com
for a retailer near you.
*English-garden-look floral, striped,
checked, and solid cotton fabrics in
a wide range of colors for every room
in the house. Coordinated pillows,
bedding, wallpaper, and trims.*

MULBERRY HOME
Call 800-453-3563 to locate
a retailer near you.
www.mulberryhome.com
*Lovely heavy linens, faded colors,
and fabrics with stately home appeal.*

OSBORNE AND LITTLE, INC.
(USA Trade Contact)
90 Commerce Road
Stamford, CT 09602
Call 203-359-1500 or visit
www.osborneandlittle.com
to locate a retailer near you.
*Fabric and wallpaper designs to help
you achieve true British style.*

THE PILLOWRY
132 East 61st Street
New York, NY 10021
212-308-1630
*Pillows in many styles made to
order, including silk, tapestry,
needlepoint, embroidery, and
knotted rug style.*

SCALAMANDRÉ
Call 212-980-3888 or visit
www.scalamandre.com for
a complete list of North
American showrooms.
*Opulent fabrics from around
the globe to lend your home
that world-traveler look.*

TRUSTWORTHY STUDIOS
P.O. Box 1109
Plymouth, MA 02362
www.trustworth.com
*Reproduction wallpaper and borders,
lighting, needlework, and other
accessories in the English Arts
and Crafts style.*

PAINT

DEFINE BY DESIGN
817-843-9558
www.definebydesign.com
*Faux and decorative finishes from
traditional to whimsical.*

FARROW & BALL
+44 1202 876141
www.farrow-ball.com
*Subtle paint colors with strange
names, National Trust paint ranges,
also papers, varnishes, and stains.*

JANOVIC
1150 Third Avenue
New York, NY 10021
800-772-4381
www.janovic.com
*Quality paints from a wide variety
of makers.*

OLD-FASHIONED MILK
PAINT COMPANY
436 Main Street
P.O. Box 222
Groton, MA 01450
478-448-6336
www.milkpaint.com
Paints made from natural pigments.

PRATT AND LAMBERT
HISTORIC PAINTS
Visit www.prattandlambert.com
to find a retail outet near you.
*150-year-old producer of top-of-
the-line paints.*

STULB'S OLD VILLAGE
PAINT
P.O. Box 1030
Fort WA, PA 19034
215-654-1770
*Vintage paint colors for furniture,
walls, and woodwork.*

HEATING AND FIREPLACES

ARCHITECTURAL
PANELING, INC.
979 Third Avenue
New York, NY 10022
212-371-9632
*Reproduction fireplaces, paneling,
and moldings.*

DANNY ALESSANDRO, LTD.
Edwin Jackson, Inc.
307 East 60th Street
New York, NY 10022
212-421-1928
*Fine fireplace mantels and
accessories.*

KITCHENS, BATHS, TILES

CLAWFOOT SUPPLY
957 Western Avenue
Covington, KY 41011
877-682-4192
www.clawfootsupply.com
*Complete supply of authentic
reproduction clawfoot tubs, pedestal
and console sinks, Topaz copper
soaking tubs, and more.*

CROWN POINT CABINETRY
153 Charlestown Road
Claremont, NH 03743
800-999-4994
www.crown-point.com
Custom cabinets for kitchen and bath.

DESIGNS IN TILE
P.O. Box 358
Mount Shasta, CA 96067
530-926-2629
www.designsintile.com
*Restored and new customized tiles,
including William Morris designs.*

HANDCRAFT TILE, INC.
1126 Yosemite Drive
Milpitas, CA 95035
877-262-1140
www.handcrafttile.com
Antique and reproduction tiles.

IKEA
1800 East McConnor Parkway
Schaumburg, IL 60173
Call 800-434-4532 or visit
www.ikea.com for the store
nearest you.
*Inexpensive, cheerful furniture and
furnishings, including good-looking
kitchen designs.*

KALLISTA
444 Highland Drive
Mailstop 032
Kohler, WI 53044
888-4-KALLISTA
www.kallistainc.com
*Luxury bathroom products;
mahogany tub surrounds, sleek and
modern fixtures, and much more.*

STONE PANELS
1725 Sandy Lake Road
Carrollton, TX 75006
972-446-1776 or 800-328-6275
www.stonepanels.com
*Stone surfaces, from limestone
to granite to marble.*

VINTAGE PLUMBING
9645 Sylvia Avenue
Northridge, CA 91324
818-772-1721
www.vintageplumbing.com
*Original and restored to perfection
bathroom antiques, including pull-
chain toilets and clawfoot bathtubs.*

FITTINGS/HARDWARE

ANTIQUE HARDWARE
AND HOME
19 Buckingham Plantation Road
Blufton, SC 29910
800-422-9982
www.antiquehardware.com
*Unusual and antique hardware
and fixtures.*

HARRINGTON BRASSWORKS
7 Pearl Court
Allendale, NJ 07401
201-818-1300
www.harringtonbrassworks.com
*Brass fixtures for kitchen and home,
including period reproductions.*

P.E. GUERIN
23 Jane Street
New York, NY 10014
212-243-5270
www.peguerin.com
*Decorative hardware, including
reproduction ironmongery.*

KOHLER
Locations throughout U.S.
800-456-4537
www.kohlerco.com
*Wide range of bathtub, sink,
and bathroom accessories.*

WATERWORKS
23 West Putnam Avenue
Greenwich, CT 06830
800-998-BATH
www.waterworks.com
*Fine fixtures, cabinets, lighting,
and fittings.*

ROSES

48 LONG STEMS
888-264-4154
www.48longstems.com
*Glorious prices for glorious quantities
of fresh roses, ordered online and
delivered to your doorstep.*

CREDITS

KEY: a=above, b=below, r=right, l=left, c=center.
All photographs by Chris Tubbs

Endpapers Matthew and Miranda Eden's home in Wiltshire; **page 1** designer Emily Todhunter's holiday home in the Peak District; **2** the Norfolk home of Geoff and Gilly Newberry of Bennison Fabrics; **3** John Martin Robinson's house in Lancashire; **4–5** Leslie Geddes-Brown and Hew Stevenson's Suffolk house; **6–7** the Norfolk home of Geoff and Gilly Newberry of Bennison Fabrics; **8–9** Ros Byam Shaw's house in Devon; **9** Julia and Michael Pruskin's family home; **10** Ben Pentreath's Georgian flat in Bloomsbury; **10–11** Simon and Antonia Johnson's home in Somerset; **12–13** Justin and Eliza Meath-Baker's house in the West Country; **14–21** Philip and Catherine Mould's house in Oxfordshire; **22–27** Simon and Diana Sieff's home in Devon; **28–35** Justin and Eliza Meath-Baker's house in the West Country; **36–41** designer Emily Todhunter's holiday home in the Peak District; **42al & 43a** Justin and Eliza Meath-Baker's house in the West Country; **42bl** Philip and Catherine Mould's house in Oxfordshire; **42br** designer Emily Todhunter's holiday home in the Peak District; **42ar & 43b** Simon and Diana Sieff's home in Devon; **43c** the Norfolk home of Geoff and Gilly Newberry of Bennison Fabrics; **44a, 44c, & 45cr** Philip and Catherine Mould's house in Oxfordshire; **44b** designer Emily Todhunter's holiday home in the Peak District; **45ar** Matthew and Miranda Eden's home in Wiltshire; **45al, 45bl, & 45br** Justin and Eliza Meath-Baker's house in the West Country; **46–47** Powers house, London; **48–53** Raffaella Barker's house in Norfolk; **54–61** Julia and Michael Pruskin's family home; **62–67** Matthew and Miranda Eden's home in Wiltshire; **68–75 & 76** Matthew and Miranda Eden's home in Wiltshire; **77al & br** Julia and Michael Pruskin's family home; **77bl** designer Emily Todhunter's holiday home in the Peak District; **77ar** Matthew and Miranda Eden's home in Wiltshire; **78al, 79c, & 79b** Powers house, London; **78cl** Ros Byam Shaw's house in Devon; **78bl & 79a** Raffaella Barker's house in Norfolk; **78br** Julia and Michael Pruskin's family home; **80–81** Annabel Grey's Norfolk cottage; **82–89** Ros Byam Shaw's house in Devon; **90–95** Annabel Grey's Norfolk cottage; **96–103** Elizabeth Baer's early Georgian home; **104–109, 110al, & 110ar** the Norfolk home of Geoff and Gilly Newberry of Bennison Fabrics; **110bl & 111a** Ros Byam Shaw's house in Devon; **110br** Raffaella Barker's house in Norfolk; **111c** the Norfolk home of Geoff and Gilly Newberry of Bennison Fabrics; **111b** Elizabeth Baer's early Georgian home; **112a** Annabel Grey's Norfolk cottage; **112c & 113cl** the Norfolk home of Geoff and Gilly Newberry of Bennison Fabrics; **112b & 113br** Elizabeth Baer's early Georgian home; **113al** Julia and Michael Pruskin's family home; **113bl** Ros Byam Shaw's house in Devon; **113ar** Hotel Endsleigh; **114–123** Leslie Geddes-Brown and Hew Stevenson's Suffolk house; **124–129** Simon and Antonia Johnson's home in Somerset; **130–135** Hotel Endsleigh; **144–149** John Martin Robinson's house in Lancashire; **150a, 150c, 151cl, & 151bl** Leslie Geddes-Brown and Hew Stevenson's Suffolk house; **150b** Hotel Endsleigh; **151al** The Children's Cottage Company; **151br, 152ar, & 152cr** Simon and Antonia Johnson's home in Somerset; **152br** Leslie Geddes-Brown and Hew Stevenson's Suffolk house; **153a** John Martin Robinson's house in Lancashire; **153c & 153b** Hotel Endsleigh; **154–155** George Carter's Norfolk farmhouse; **156–161** Nicolette Le Pelley's home in London; **162–167** Ben Pentreath's Georgian flat in Bloomsbury; **168–175** George Carter's Norfolk farmhouse; **176–181** the London flat of Roger Jones of Sibyl Colefax and John Fowler; **182al** Ben Pentreath's Georgian flat in Bloomsbury; **182ar** George Carter's Norfolk farmhouse; **182bl** the London flat of Roger Jones of Sibyl Colefax and John Fowler; **182br** Hotel Endsleigh; **183a & 183b** the London flat of Roger Jones of Sibyl Colefax and John Fowler; **182c** Matthew and Miranda Eden's home in Wiltshire; **184a & 185al** the London flat of Roger Jones of Sibyl Colefax and John Fowler; **184c** George Carter's Norfolk farmhouse; **184b, 185cl, & 185br** Nicolette Le Pelley's home in London; **185bl & 185ar** Ben Pentreath's Georgian flat in Bloomsbury.

Architects, designers, and business owners whose work is featured in this book:

ANNABEL GREY

+44 7860 500356
annabel.grey@btinternet.com
www.annabelgrey.com
also at:
The Old Stables (shop)
Bayfield Hall
Near Holt
Norfolk
Pages 80–81, 90–95, 112a

BEN PENTREATH

Working Group Design
49 Lamb's Conduit Street
London WC1N 3NG
+44 20 7430 2424
fax +44 20 7430 2924
www.working-group.co.uk
Pages 10, 162–167, 182al, 185bl, 185ar

BENNISON

The Fine Arts Building
232 East 59th Street
New York, NY 10022
and
8264 Melrose Avenue
Los Angeles, CA 90046
www.bennisonfabrics.com
*Pages 2, 6–7, 43c, 104–109, 110al, 110ar,
111c, 112c, 113cl*

THE CHILDREN'S COTTAGE
COMPANY

Devon
+44 1363 772061
fax +44 1363 777868
www.play-houses.com
and
Sanctuary Garden Offices
Devon
+44 1363 772061
fax +44 1363 777868
www.sanctuarygardenoffices.com
Pages 78ar, 136–143, 151al, 151ar, 152al, 152bl

ELIZABETH BAER TEXTILES

telephone/fax +44 1225 866136
dbaer@onetel.com
in addition:
Juliana, period curtains relined and
refurbished +44 7769 560918
Michael Leeson, all decorating and paper
hanging +44 7768 061769
Baer & Ingram wallpapers and fabrics,
+44 1373 812552
Pages 96–103, 111b, 112b, 113br

GEORGE CARTER GARDEN DESIGN

grcarter@easynet.co.uk
The Engine House, in the grounds of
George Carter's house, is available as
a holiday property through
www.statelyholidayhomes.com
Pages 154–155, 168–175, 182ar, 184c

HOTEL ENDSLEIGH

Milton Abbot
Tavistock
Devon
+44 1822 870000
fax +44 1822 870578
mail@hotelendsleigh.com
www.hotelendsleigh.com
Pages 113ar, 130–135, 150b, 153c, 153b, 182br

HOUSE & GARDEN ADDRESSES

Free online directory for interior and
garden design and decoration, with
over 3,000 companies listed.
telephone/fax +44 20 7221 6600
info@houseandgardenaddresses.co.uk
www.houseandgardenaddresses.co.uk
Pages 156–161, 184b, 185cl, 185br

JOHN MARTIN ROBINSON

Historic Buildings Consultants
8 Doughty Mews
London WC1N 2PG
+44 20 7831 4398
www.hbcconsultants.com
Pages 3, 144–149, 153a

JUDD STREET GALLERY

www.juddstreetgallery.com
Pages 46–47, 54–61, 78al, 79c, 79b

PHILIP MOULD'S HISTORICAL
PORTRAITS LIMITED

+44 20 7499 6818
fax +44 20 7495 0793
philip@historicalportraits.com
www.historicalportraits.com
also involved in this project:
Keith and Jane Riley, historical and
restoration design +44 1608 644992
info@keyantiques.com
Pages 14–21, 42bl, 44a, 44c, 45cr

PRUSKIN GALLERY

73 Kensington Church Street
London W8 4BG
+44 20 7937 1994
and
96 Portland Road
London W11 4LQ
+44 20 7727 9062
Pages 9, 62–67, 77al, 77br, 78br, 113al

RAFFAELLA BARKER

For location work please contact:
raffaella.barker@btinternet.com
www.locationpartnership.com
Property number HC601
Interior decorating by Annabel Grey
(see above)
Pages 48–53, 78bl, 79a, 110br

ROGER JONES

Sibyl Colefax and John Fowler
39 Brook Street
London W1K 4JE
+44 20 7493 2231
fax +44 20 7499 9721
roger.jones@sibylcolefax.com
www.colefaxantiques.com
Pages 176–181, 182bl, 183a, 183b, 184a, 185al

SIEFF INTERIORS

+44 20 7978 2422
fax +44 20 7978 2423
sieff@sieff.co.uk
www.sieff.co.uk
Pages 22–27, 42ar, 43b

TODHUNTER EARLE INTERIORS

+44 20 7349 9999
interiors@todhunterearle.com
www.todhunterearle.com
Pages 1, 36–41, 42br, 44b, 77bl

INDEX

Page numbers in *italic* refer to illustrations and their captions

A

Agas *14–15*, 22, 26, 67, 71,
  82–3, *117*, *125*, *146*, 150
Anthony Redmile Antiques *25*
antiquities 184
apartments *see* flats
Art Deco 67
Artemide *33*
Arts and Crafts 43, 51, 67
  furniture *22–3*, *25*, *41*, *83*, *126*
  mirrors *60*
  textiles *63*, 67
attic bedrooms *20–1*, *34*

B

Baer, Elizabeth and Derek 71,
  97–103
balance, classic style 183
Barker, Raffaella 48–53, 76
bathrooms: Bloomsbury flat *167*
  Bloomsbury house 58, *61*
  Cheshire gamekeeper's lodge
    40
  Columbine Hall 122, *122*
  Devon country house 142, *143*
  Endsleigh 135
  Exmoor farmhouse *26*
  Kensington flat *181*
  Norfolk cottage *95*
  Norfolk rectory *52*, *108*
  Notting Hill row house *160*
  Oxfordshire manor house *20*
  Severn Valley farmhouse 35,
    35
  Somerset house *129*
  Southwold house *67*
  Tudor house *89*
  Wiltshire house *75*
bathstore.com *40*
Bawden, Edward *54*, 58, *60*
Bedford, Duke and Duchess of
  132, 135
bedrooms: Bloomsbury flat *166*,
  166
  Bloomsbury house 58, *59*
  Bradford-on-Avon house
    102–3, 103
  Cheshire gamekeeper's lodge
    38, *41*
  Columbine Hall *122*, *123*
  Devon country house 142,
    142, 143
  Endsleigh *134–5*
  Exmoor farmhouse *26–7*

Kensington flat *178–81*, 181
Lancashire country house *149*
neo-Georgian house *173*, *175*
Norfolk cottage *92*, *94–5*
Norfolk rectory *52–3*, 108,
  108–9
Notting Hill row house *160–1*
Oxfordshire manor house *19*,
  20–1
Severn Valley farmhouse
  32–3, *34*
Somerset house *129*
Southwold house *66–7*
Tudor house *86*, *88–9*
Wiltshire house *68–71*, *74*
beds, country-house style 153
Bell, Ken *129*
Bennett, Peter *86–7*
Bennison 86, *104*, *106*, 107
Bennison, Geoffrey 107–8, *107*,
  108
Beuys, Joseph 76
Biba 48, *48*
Binney, Jennifer *93*
Bloomsbury 54–61, 162–7
Blossfeldt, Karl 129
Body, Eve 128, *128*
books 58, *58*, 79, *86–7*, *94*, *116*,
  160, 170, *177*
Boontje, Tord 48
boot rooms *134*, 149, 153
Bradford-on-Avon 96–103
brick floors 121
Burra, Edward *127*

C

Calke Abbey 122
candlesticks 172, 184
Canovas *89*
carpets 38, *41*
Carr, John 146
Carter, George 9, 118, 168–75,
  184
ceilings, proportions 183
ceramics 44, *57*, *92*, 112, *163*, 184
chandeliers *40*
Charles II, King 15
Cheshire 36–41
Chesterfield sofas *16*, 153
china *see* ceramics
Christensen, Helena *49*
classic style 155–85
Coalport *90*
Colefax and Fowler 10, 68, *74*,
  86, *88–9*, *149*, *167*, 176

colors: Cheshire gamekeeper's
    lodge 41
  eccentric style 76
  neo-Georgian house 170
  Norfolk rectory 48, 51–2, *51*
  plain English style 43
Columbine Hall, Suffolk 9,
  116–23, *117–22*
cork tiles 37, 38
Cornforth, John 112
cottage orné style 132–4
country-house style 114–53
Crag Hall estate, Cheshire 37
crewelwork *24*, *25*, *63*
Crowley, Ambrose *121*
curtains: antique linen sheets 98
  Bloomsbury house *54*
  Bradford-on-Avon house
    96–7, 103
  Cheshire gamekeeper's lodge
    41
  Exmoor farmhouse *24*, 25, *26*
  Norfolk rectory *50*, 52
  plain English style 43
  Wiltshire house *74*
cushions 153

D

Day, Lucienne 94
Denny, Thomas *126*
Derby, Earl and Countess of
  37
Devon 82–9, 130–5, 136–43
dining rooms: Bloomsbury
    house 58
  Bradford-on-Avon house
    96–7, 98, *99*, 103
  Columbine Hall *118–19*,
    120–1, 121
  country-house style 153
  Devon country house *139*, 142
  Exmoor farmhouse 25, *25*
  Lancashire country house
    144–5
  neo-Georgian house *170–1*
  Norfolk rectory 50, 51, 52
  Severn Valley farmhouse 30,
    33
  Somerset house *126*
  Tudor house *84–5*
  Wiltshire house *70–1*
distemper 54
Domenichino *161*
drawing rooms: Columbine
  Hall 122

Devon country house *140–1*,
  142
Endsleigh *132–3*, 135
Exmoor farmhouse *24*, 25
Lancashire country house *148*
neo-Georgian house *168–9*,
  172, *172*
dressers *91*, 94
Ducci *121*

E

eccentric style 47–79
Ede, Jim 44
Eden, Catherine 71
Eden, Matthew and Miranda
  68–75, 79
Eden, Robin 68, *70*, 71, 98
eiderdowns 112
elm floorboards 30, *32*
Endsleigh, Devon 10, 130–5,
  130–5, 153
English rose style 81–113

F

fabrics: antique 98, *100–3*
  Arts and Crafts *63*, 67
  Bennison 107
  classic style 184
  country-house style 150
  English rose style 111
  Indian *20*
  plain English style 44
  Uzbekistani textiles *41*
family rooms 58, *58*
Farrow and Ball *25*, *160*
filing cabinets 30, 33, *34*
fireplaces: Bloomsbury flat *162*,
  166
  Bradford-on-Avon house 98,
    98
  Cheshire gamekeeper's lodge
    38, *39*
  Columbine Hall *118*
  Devon country house *137*
  Kensington flat 178, *179*
  Lancashire country house
    144, 146, *148*, 149
  neo-Georgian house *169*
  Norfolk rectory *50*
  Notting Hill row house *158*
  Oxfordshire manor house
    18–19
  Severn Valley farmhouse *31*,
    33, *33*

Somerset house *127, 128*
Tudor house 84, 86
flagstone floors *29*, 30, 43, *70–1, 126*
flats 162–7, *162–7*, 176–81, *176–81*
floors: brick 121
  carpets 38, *41*
  cork tiles *37*, 38
  country-house style 150
  floor paint *48*, 76
  rubber 35, *35*
  seagrass matting *160*
  slate 156
  stone *29*, 30, 43, *70–1, 126*
  terracotta tiles 93, *93, 105, 117*
  travertine *64–5*, 65
  wooden *19*, 20, 30, *32, 34*, 43
flowers 112, *130–1*, 153
Forte, Rocco 134
"found objects" 44
Fowler, John 10, *54*, 111, 112, 115, 150, 176
Fraser, Maurice 156–61
Fulham Pottery *64*, 67, *92*
furniture: classic style 183
  country-house style 150
  English rose style 111
  modern furniture 44
  old furniture 44

G

Gainsborough, Thomas 15–16
gamekeeper's lodge, Cheshire 36–41, *36–41*
garden rooms 108, *108*
gardens: Cheshire gamekeeper's lodge *37*
  and English rose style 111
  Lancashire country house 149
  neo-Georgian house 168–70, *168, 175*
  Norfolk cottage 90, 93
  Norfolk rectory 104, *104*
  Oxfordshire manor house *15*, 19, 20
  Southwold house *63*, 65
Gaudier-Brzeska, Henri 44
Geddes-Brown, Leslie 9, 117–22
George VI, King *129*
Georgian Group 145
Georgian houses 54–61, 96–103, 104–9, 144–9, 183
Gibbs, Christopher 129
Gibbs, James *145*, 146
Gothic style *21*, 51
Green, Penny *125*
Grey, Annabel 48–51, *50*, 52,

76, 90–5, 112
Gruau, René 67
Gryn, David *48*

H

Haigh, Michael 149
halls: Bradford-on-Avon house 97
  Cheshire gamekeeper's lodge *37*, 38
  Endsleigh *130–1*
  Kensington flat *181*
  Norfolk rectory 51
  Notting Hill row house 156
  Wiltshire house *68–9*
Hamilton Weston 149
Hammond, Hermione 58, *59*
Hawkins, Jeremiah 30, 35
Heal's *62, 82–3*
Hepworth, Barbara 44
Heveningham Hall, Suffolk *146*
Hird, John 146
Hogarth, William 20, 184
Hone, Peter 68
hotels 130–5, *130–5*
House & Garden Addresses, 159–60

I

Indian textiles *20*
Iron Bed Company *86*

J

Johnson, Arabella *84*
Johnson, Simon and Antonia 125–9
Jones, Inigo 183
Jones, Roger 10, 176–81
Judd Street Gallery Pattern Papers *54*, 60, 79

K

Kensington 176–81
Kettle's Yard, Cambridge 44
Kiff, Ken *129*
Kime, Robert *126*, 129
Kirkpatrick, Margaret *92*, 94
kitchens: Bloomsbury flat *164*
  Bloomsbury house 56–7, 58
  Bradford-on-Avon house *100*
  Cheshire gamekeeper's lodge *36*
  Columbine Hall *116–17*, 121–2
  Devon country house *138*
  Exmoor farmhouse *22*, 25
  Lancashire country house *146*

Norfolk cottage *90–1*
Norfolk rectory 51, *51, 104–5*
Notting Hill row house 156, *156–7*
Oxfordshire manor house *14–15*
Severn Valley farmhouse *30*, 33
Somerset house *124–5*
Southwold house *62*, 65–7
Tudor house *82–3*
Wiltshire house *71*
Knight, Winifred 58, *59*
Knight-Bruce, Robin and Catrina 136–43
Knorr, Cheryl 159

L

Lamb, Alan *145*
Lancashire 144–9
Lancaster, Nancy 10, 68, *74*, 86, 112, 115, 142, 150
landings: Bradford-on-Avon house *101*
  Norfolk cottage *93*
  Norfolk rectory *52*
  Wiltshire house *72*, 74
Langley, Batty 146
Le Pelley, Nicolette 156–61, 184
leather upholstery *16–17*, 44, *85*
Lelievre 149
libraries: Bloomsbury house 58
  Columbine Hall 122
  Endsleigh *132*
  Lancashire country house *146, 147*
  neo-Georgian house *174–5*
lighting: Cheshire gamekeeper's lodge *40*
  Norfolk rectory *48*, 49
  Severn Valley farmhouse *30*, 33
  Wiltshire house *69*
limestone 43
limewash *48*, 121–2, *145*
Litvinoff and Fawcett *33*
living rooms: Bloomsbury flat *162, 164, 164–5, 166–7*
  Bloomsbury house *54–5*, 58–60
  Bradford-on-Avon house 98, *100*, 103
  Cheshire gamekeeper's lodge 38, *38–9*
  Endsleigh *134*
  Exmoor farmhouse *25*
  Kensington flat *176–7*, 181
  Norfolk cottage *94*
  Norfolk rectory *48–9*, 51,

106–7, 107
  Notting Hill row house 156, *158–9*
  Oxfordshire manor house *18–19*
  Severn Valley farmhouse *29*, 33
  Somerset house 127–8, *128*
  Southwold house *63*, 67
  Wiltshire house *72–3*
  see also drawing rooms
London 54–61, 156–61, 162–7, 176–81
Ludwig, King of Bavaria 76
Lutyens, Edwin 70
Lycett Green, Endellion *49*
Lyster, Polly *88–9*

M

McGregor, Archie *73*
Mankin, Ian *159, 164*
manor house, Oxfordshire 14–21, *14–21*
Marx, Enid *54*
matchboarding *27*, 43, *156–7*
matting, seagrass *160*
Meath-Baker, Eliza and Justin 7, 9–10, *29–35*, 43, 44
minimalism 44
mirrors, Arts and Crafts *60*
Mocha pottery *163*
Monmouth, Duke of *83*, 86
Moore, Henry 44
morning rooms *107*
Morris, Charles *164*
Morris, William 43, 74
Mould, Catherine and Philip 15–20, 44
Muchelney Abbey 127, *129*
murals *125*

N

Native American art 129
natural materials 43, 44
neo-Georgian house 168–72, *168–75*
New Hall china 170, 184
Newberry, Frank *93*
Newberry, Gilly and Geoff 104–8
Norfolk 48–53, 90–5, 104–9, 168–75
Norris, Charles and Jenny 20
Notting Hill 156–61

O

objets trouvés 44
Oxfordshire 14–21

P

paint: distemper *54*
  floor paint *48*, 76
  limewash *48*, 121–2, *145*
  plain English style 43
Palladio, Andrea 183
paneling *129*, *166*
  17th-century 84, *84–5*
  18th-century 98, *99*
  19th-century *137*
  matchboarding *27*, 43, *156–7*
  plywood *120–1*, 122, *122*
parlors *28*
patterns, English rose style 111
Peak District 36–41
Pell Wall Hall, Somerset *177*
Pentreath, Ben 162–7, 184
Pevsner, Nikolaus *83*
pewter 44
pictures: Bloomsbury flat *163*
  Bloomsbury house 58, *59*, 60
  classic style 184
  country-house style 153
  English rose style 112
  neo-Georgian house 170
  Notting Hill row house 156
  Severn Valley farmhouse
    33–5
  Tudor 15
Piper, John 58, *60*
plain English style 13–45
plasterwork 127–8, *128*
playhouses 136, *136*
Poley, Sir John *122*
Polizzi, Olga 131–5
Pope, Alexander 183
potted plants 112
pottery *see* ceramics
Powers, Alan and Susanna
  54–61, 76, 79
Powers, William 58, *59*, 60
Prior, E. S. 51
proportions, classic style 183

Proust, Marcel 76
Pruskin, Julia and Michael
  62–7, 76, 79
Pruskin Gallery, London 67

Q

quilts 112

R

ranges *33*
Ravilious, Eric *54*, 58, *60*, 167
Ravilious, James 167
Ray Coggins Interiors,
  Bradford-on-Avon 40
Rayburn 33, *90*, 93
rectory, Norfolk 104–9, *104–9*
Regency houses 132–5, 136–43
Renaissance 183
Repton, Humphrey 132
Riley, Keith and Jane 20
Robinson, Dr. John Martin
  145–9
Roman shades 94
roses 81
Rowley Gallery *175*
rubber flooring 35, *35*

S

Schierenberg, Tai-Shan *163*, 167
screens *64*
seagrass matting *160*
Severn Valley farmhouse
  28–35, *28–35*
shades 43, 94, *165*
shelving *56–7*, *86–7*
Shepard, E. H. *74*
Sieff, Diana and Simon 7, 22–6,
  43
sitting rooms *see* drawing
  rooms; living rooms
slate floors 156
Smith, George *63*

Smith, Melvyn 118–22, *121*,
  122
Soane, Sir John 155, *177*, 178
sofas, Chesterfield *16*, 153
Soliz, Cecile Johnson 135
Somerset 124–9
Sorrell, Alan 58, *60*
Southwold 62–7
staircases: Bloomsbury house *60*
  Cheshire gamekeeper's lodge
    38
  Columbine Hall *121*
  Devon country house *141*
  Exmoor farmhouse *22–3*
  Norfolk rectory *48*, 51–2
  Southwold house 65, *65*
  Wiltshire house *68*
Stevenson, Hew 9, 118–22
stone floors *29*, 30, 43, *70–1*,
  126
Stuart Interiors *129*
studies 33, 52, 143
Suffolk 116–23
suzanis 41, *41*
symmetry, classic style 183

T

Taunton Antiques Market *141*
terracotta tiles 93, *93*, *105*, *117*
ticking 100
tiles: cork *37*, 38
  murals *125*
  terracotta 93, *93*, *105*, *117*
T.K. Maxx *90*
Todhunter, Emily 7, 37–41, 43
Todhunter Earle 37
toys, vintage *32*
travertine floors *64–5*, 65
Tree, Ronald 68, *74*
Tudor house 82–9, *82–9*
Tudor paintings 15
Twentieth Century Society 57

U

upholstery, leather *16–17*, 44, *85*
Uzbekistani textiles *41*

V

Vanbrugh, Sir John 155, *175*
Viaduct *33*
Vincent, Giles 178
Voewood House, Norfolk 51

W

wallpapers: Bennison *104*, *107*
  English rose style 111
  Hamilton Weston *149*
  Regency 135, *135*
Watts, George Frederick *73*
Waugh, Evelyn 153
Wedgwood 184
wet rooms *51*
white, plain English style 43
Wilson, Scottie *126*
Wiltshire 68–75
windows: plain English style 43
  proportions 183
  see also curtains
Windsor Castle 15
wooden floors *19*, 20, 30, *32*,
  34, 43
  see also paneling
Working Group 164
Wren, Christopher 72, 163
Wyatt, James *146*
Wyatt, Jeffrey 132
Wyatt family *146*
Wyndham, Melissa *148*

Y

Yeoward, William *132*

ACKNOWLEDGMENTS

The team at Ryland Peters & Small have been, without exception, supportive and constructive. I would like to thank, in particular, Alison Starling who first championed the idea for the book, Toni Kay who designed it, Clare Double who edited it, and Emily Westlake, whose charm and diplomacy were invaluable when organizing the photography. Chris Tubbs was a pleasure to work with, and took beautiful photographs. I would also like to thank all the owners of the houses for their time and their help. Some were already friends, others were a joy to meet and talk to. Lastly, thank you to Professor Steven Parissien, whose scholarly advice was much appreciated.